The Meaning of Pastoral Care

CARROLL A. WISE

With Revisions and Additions by

John E. Hinkle, Jr.

MEYER
STONE
BOOKS

Published in the United States by Meyer-Stone Books,
a division of Meyer, Stone, and Company, Inc.,
2014 South Yost Avenue, Bloomington, IN 47403.
Telephone: 812-333-0313

Cover design: Carol Evans-Smith

Typesetting output: T_EXSource, Houston

Manufactured in the United States of America
93 92 91 90 89 89   5 4 3 2 1

Library of Congress Cataloging in Publication Data

Wise, Carroll A.
  The meaning of pastoral care.

  Bibliography: p.
  Includes index.
  1. Pastoral theology.   I. Hinkle, John E.
II. Title.
BV4011.W55   1989   253   88-43047
ISBN 0-940989-46-8 (pbk)
ISBN 0-940989-51-4 (library binding)

*To those persons
to whom I have been privileged to stand
in a relationship of pastoral care,
and to those students
with whom I have been privileged to enter
into a mutual teaching-learning relationship*

Contents

Preface to the 1966 Edition

CERTAIN PROBLEMS IN PASTORAL CARE have been emerging during the past four decades, whether the setting has been a parish, a hospital, or a theological seminary. Perhaps the central problem has been this: What does pastoral care have to offer persons, and how is it given? There has been some real questioning of the value of offering the intellectual, liturgical, and ecclesiastical structures of religion in certain circumstances, and there have been answers pro and con. Some theologians have joined pastors in asserting the value of offering theological ideas as part of pastoral care. But the real question has remained. How and under what conditions do the various structures of religion become meaningful to persons?

This book is not an attempt to do away with the structures of religion. Obviously that would be foolishness. It is an attempt to show that structures are undergirded by a deeper element, an element that has often been called spirit. This book cuts across certain traditional approaches and elaborates the conviction that relationships are fundamental to pastoral care. This has been a neglected dimension, but it appears to be the basis for dealing with certain pressing questions. Although relationship is often casually assumed, and then lightly dismissed, it is at once the desperate need of persons and the essential quality of the gospel. Many questions in pastoral care are hardly intelligible unless we are constantly aware of the distinction between the structures of the faith and relationships within the faith, and unless we understand on which level we are thinking. The emphasis of this book is on the meaning of pastoral relationships as the basis for the communication of the gospel. This book is also an attempt to relate the theological dimension of pastoral care to the personal dimension. Because of the nature of the problems involved, one can go only so far with verbal formulations. I make no claim to have gone the limit. However, I would stress the idea that any real integration of the two dimensions occurs within the person of the pastor when form and spirit find a workable and working unity in the depths of the pastor's being.

As the title indicates, this is not a work on the techniques of pastoral care. It is rather an attempt to interpret the meaning of pastoral care, and to set pastoral care within the context of the gospel. To the extent that this book has grasped the real issues and processes, it will have contributed a basis for judging techniques. The emphasis is more on the dimensions of being and knowing, in the direct personal sense, than of doing.

The concept of pastoral care elaborated here is more inclusive than the usual one, which confines pastoral care to dealing with persons in certain kinds of life crises. The concern is with pastoral care in relation to the growth of persons, and with the psychological aspects of growth in relation to pastoral care. Genuine pastoral care in today's world cannot afford to be otherwise.

This book owes much to more people than I can at any moment consciously bring to mind. Teachers, colleagues, and students have contributed much. Above all, I am indebted to persons with whom I have stood in the pastoral relationship. It has been my privilege to give portions of the book as lectures in conferences for pastors, in theological seminaries, and to groups of laypersons. I have profited from their reactions and comments. More specifically I would like to express appreciation for the intellectual encounters and personal fellowship that have come through membership in the faculty of the Garrett Theological Seminary. This is a stimulating relationship in which to live and work, made all the more so by the cross-fertilization of inquisitive students who carry pollen from one professorial mind to another, to the enrichment of all. Two of my colleagues, Dr. William Hordern and Dr. Morris Taggart, have read parts of the manuscript and have given valuable suggestions.

One person whom I wish to mention in gratitude is Dr. Anton T. Boisen, not because he is the source of any of the ideas in this book, though he may be, but rather because he started me on a long experience of clinical pastoral training. He constantly insisted that his students learn to read the human document.

My thanks to Miss Marilyn Butt, who efficiently put the manuscript into final form. And my gratitude to my wife, Addiene G. Wise, for constant inspiration and support.

Carroll A. Wise
April 1966

Preface to the Revised Edition

PROFOUND CULTURAL, SOCIAL, AND TECHNOLOGICAL CHANGES have swept over humankind and the human mind since Wise gave us the original version of *The Meaning of Pastoral Care* more than twenty years ago. Joseph Campbell characterizes this historical period as one in which "we are at this moment participating in one of the very greatest leaps of the human spirit to a knowledge not only of outside nature but also of our own deep inward mystery."[1] Outer changes signal a need for inner change by way of response. Jesus spoke of the need to discern the signs of the times as a key element in spiritual awareness. Those who failed to discern the signs of the times were rebuked. The New Testament theme of eschatology, the coming into being of the new age to which Jesus was pointing, clearly applies to this post-modern era as well. One of our tasks in such times is to discern the signs of the times in this new age with a view to understanding what God is doing. This republication of the work of Wise constitutes an effort to place his thought in the context of the post-modern world.

Wise was writing at a time of transition. His thinking was at the forefront of a shift away from simply and only traditional approaches to pastoral care uninformed by the new knowledge available in the social and personality sciences. He wrote at the cutting edge of a movement to integrate new knowledge from the personality sciences into theological and pastoral understandings of pastoral care and counseling. He wrote as a clinically enlightened, theologically grounded, and pastorally motivated professor of pastoral psychology and counseling. He focused on the theological-psychological heart of pastoral care. A result was this classic statement on pastoral care.

Works that have the stature of a classic should be republished with as little change as is feasible for the new context. The mind and thought of the original text should shine forth for the reader to encounter in pristine form. Hence Wise's portion of this text has been modified only in terms of the conventions of current language use, with particular concern for gender-referenced pronouns. At the same time, the cultural and social changes noted above simply cannot be ignored in a book as important as this one.

The strategy I have employed, then, is to retain Carroll's thought as is, but to add a chapter that gives indications of ways in which readers may want and need to revise the material in terms of the their own context and concerns in today's world. Along the way in that chapter I review biblical, sociocultural, psychological, and pastoral care issues that suggest possibilities for revision of the Wise model of pastoral care, while seeking to retain the lasting message of Wise. The bibliographical references for that chapter are rather extensive, in part as an effort to update the bibliography for the entire book.

One intent of the final chapter is to set the Wise emphasis upon relationship as the key to pastoral care in the context of the "mighty multicultural frame."[2] The multicultural context of Pentecost is added to the individual and communal frame of Incarnation to enlarge the biblical image and to broaden the theological theme. The multicultural, inclusive, and mystical dimensions of Pentecost provide a proper setting for enduring aspects of the work of Wise in the context of the unprecedented expansion of the human spirit occurring in today's world.

The question that Wise is addressing in this text is as pressingly poignant now as it was twenty years ago, perhaps more so. The question that guides his thinking is, "How and under what conditions do the various structures of religion become meaningful to persons?" Moyer says to Campbell, "You are talking about a search for the meaning of life?" and Campbell responds, "No, no, no, . . . for the *experience* of being alive."[3] Wise would agree with Campbell, but would add: being alive in Christ. The focus is on experience. As Carroll writes in his preface, "The emphasis of this book is on the meaning of pastoral relationships as the basis for the communication of the gospel." The question has not changed. The context has changed. This revision seeks to address the issue of context in a manner that elaborates, extends, and in some instances critiques the model of pastoral care presented by Wise. The volume will have served its purpose if readers join in the process of "re-contexting" the thoughts of Wise on pastoral care in their own context and ministry.

A word of appreciation is due to David Meyer for his encouragement in the initiation of this project. Addiene Wise generously and gladly facilitated the contract and copyright concerns. John Eagleson has made helpful suggestions and given considerable energy to technical aspects of this edition. Pam Holliman and Greg Hinkle reviewed the final chapter and contributed suggestions for improvement of the text. Paul Hessert's abiding influence lies in these pages as well. A word of acknowledgement and appreciation must go to the many who have shared themselves through relationships of love with this writer, both within and across cultures, participating in the lively essence of the experience of the gospel in that process. In particular parishioners and colleagues in the Philippine Islands, Filipinos all, who long ago taught this writer the meaning of the gospel of love in another culture, are remembered. As Wise says, the inner meaning of the gospel is communicated through loving relationships in experiences deeper than words. These experiences, while shaped and formed by cultural and linguistic conventions, can be known in any culture. But the experience of love that transcends cultural boundaries is especially moving, as the testimony of the woman at the well in Samaria so aptly demonstrates. And finally, this book is dedicated to all those who have either had such experience and know the meaning of the gospel, or who yearn for that profound level of meaningful human existence for their own lives.

John E. Hinkle, Jr.
November 1988

NOTES

1. Joseph Campbell, *The Power of Myth*, ed. Betty Sue Flowers (New York: Doubleday, 1988), p. xviii.
2. Ibid.
3. Ibid., p. xvi.

≺ 1 ≻

The Biblical Basis of Pastoral Care

THE LIVING MODEL of pastoral care for the Christian minister is the person and work of Jesus as revealed in the Gospels. Abstract concepts of pastoral care have been developed through the centuries under such labels as "pastoral theology," but these concepts have been powerless to create effective pastors. Christian pastors are those who in their very persons and in their living relationships with people mediate something of the quality of being that is found in a larger measure in the revelation of Christ. This quality of being speaks, in turn, of a quality in the eternal nature of God, and of a living relationship that God offers human beings. Because it is a gift of God to humankind, its manifestation in human life speaks of the Giver. In this living relationship there are reconciliation, forgiveness, and healing that reach below the struggles of human existence into the very core of our being. Out of this relationship come insight and power for daily life. This living relationship is the context in which the Holy Spirit manifests itself. Only the presence of the Holy Spirit will save a pastor from a mechanical imitation of the model presented by Jesus — with all of the destructiveness of such imitation.

We cannot here review all the material in the New Testament out of which a Christian conception of pastoral care develops.[1] The charge that Jesus gave his disciples prior to sending them out on a mission is clear (Matt. 9:35–10:16). They were persons sent in his name, with his authority, to carry on his mission and ministry. They were to preach that the Kingdom of God was a

present potentiality waiting to be realized in human lives. They
were to heal the sick, raise the dead, cleanse the lepers, cast out
demons. In other words, they were to deal with the profound
needs of human beings as they had seen Jesus dealing with those
needs. As the disciples had received, so they were to give, freely
and in the spirit of their Master. The principle involved here
is very important. Pastors cannot give unless they have first
received. Indeed, giving and receiving are simultaneous experiences, and pastoral care is a deeply mutual undertaking.

The origin of the pastoral concept in the ancient art of shepherding is well known. In John 10 Jesus is reported to have
used the symbol as a vehicle for the interpretation of his mission, and consequently for the work of those whom he sent out.
Seward Hiltner has elaborated this concept.[2] However, this symbol cannot have the power for people today that it had in the
first century. There are other symbols more realistic to the modern mind. While recognizing the power of this symbol as Jesus
used it, we shall not make much use of it in this study, but shall
attempt to deal with the realities involved in the care of pastors for their people. One of the dangers of this symbol to the
modern mind is that it can subtly but powerfully convey the
idea of the superiority of pastors over their "sheep," whereas in
the New Testament, pastoral care is the ministry of persons who
stand in the same relationship to God as do those to whom they
minister.

A symbol more meaningful and powerful to people today is
that which St. Paul used in 2 Corinthians 5. Here the stress
is on the experience of reconciliation: God through Christ has
reconciled us to God and has given us the ministry of reconciliation. Today people are aware of conflict on many levels —
personal, social, ideational, political — and of the need for reconciliation. Indeed, a profession has been developed, that of
psychotherapy, aimed at helping persons resolve inner conflict
and become reconciled, at least in part, to themselves and to
others. Throughout this book, we shall stress the goal of reconciliation as fundamental to pastoral care.

A final New Testament passage to which we would call attention is 1 Corinthians 12:4–13:13. The burden of this passage
is first of all the charismatic nature of the ministry. It is the
exercise of gifts through the Spirit, and there are different gifts

corresponding to the different functions that need to be fulfilled in the church. But there is only one Spirit, the same Lord and God "who inspires them all in everyone." Usually the thirteenth chapter is not seen as an integral part of Paul's discussion of the ministry. But if read as a whole, without regard to the mechanics of chapter and verse, it becomes clear that Paul is pointing to a higher gift that is indispensable in any form of the ministry, and that is the gift of love. Whether this be exegesis or eisegesis, New Testament scholars will have to decide. It is true to the reality of the Christian ministry, as we shall stress in the pages ahead. For whether we preach, teach, conduct the affairs of the church, or engage in any other pastoral activity, if we have not love our ministry is nothing. This is the central problem of the pastoral ministry today.

The ministry of our Lord as recorded in the New Testament was deep, inclusive, and richly varied. For this reason there is no one symbol that fully interprets his ministry. Recently there has been great stress on Christ as the Word of God, and hence on the ministry of the Word. This is often taken to be preaching. But Christ as the Word of God implies something far more than preaching. It points to a message revealed in a life that was grounded in a profound faith in God and in a self-giving love toward human beings. It was a communication from God to humankind on a level far deeper than the verbal — the level of being. The ministry of the Word is no less a pastoral ministry than it is a preaching ministry. It is far more than the spoken word. It is manifest or frustrated in the very life of pastors as they come into living contact with other persons.

Much of the pastoral ministry is in listening, not in speaking or preaching. But listening in understanding love is no less a ministry of the Word of Love than is proclaiming the love of God from the pulpit. Indeed, preaching, except for persons with inhibition of speech, is far easier and entails less personal stress than the ministry to individuals in time of deep need. This is one reason why so many "preachers" do so little and such poor work with individuals. Had Jesus not listened to many persons with understanding love and had he not reflected deeply on what he heard, it is difficult to see how he could have created the parables, which hold up a mirror before people so that those who have eyes may see themselves as God sees them.

As a textbook on pastoral care, the record of the Gospels is both complete and incomplete. Much of what Jesus said and did is undoubtedly missing, much that we have is condensation, and much undoubtedly has been distorted in transmission. The Gospels certainly cannot be considered a textbook on pastoral care in any literal sense. There are problems encountered in pastoral care on which they have nothing directly to say.

In another sense the Gospels are a complete revelation of the meaning of pastoral care. This is because they reveal the Spirit of Jesus in relation to persons and their needs. It is also because this Spirit is in itself the manifestation of the Spirit of God. Jesus was dedicated to showing forth the love of God in his own love for people. "As the Father has sent me, so send I you" (John 20:21) was his charge to his disciples. Only those who have shared in this ministry as receivers will have any part of it to give.

The direction of the pastoral ministry of Jesus is as clear as its source. It was directed to the needs of people. The full meaning of this requires much reflection and elaboration.

Jesus was singularly free from one of the burdens of many modern pastors — the task of maintaining an institution or of administering a church. One of the disillusionments of many modern ministers is that they go into the ministry to help people, but find themselves a part of the machinery of an institution in which it seems they must use people rather than help them. Richard Niebuhr's description of the minister as a "pastoral-director" is indicative of the schizophrenic split in the professional consciousness of many ministers today.[3] Their personal identity as ministers is anything but whole. Not so with Jesus. He was free to minister to persons. Today there are movements within the ministry that are seeking to learn how to use the church for the welfare of people, to learn how individuals may be helped through the fellowship of the church, and to see the church itself as an institution that should minister rather than be ministered to. The Spirit that motivates the true pastor will always be in conflict with that spirit that glorifies the institution and makes it an end in itself.

Jesus was also singularly free from the role problems of the modern pastor.[4] This consciousness of role, the sense of conflict and confusion of roles, the uncertainty as to what role should be played and when, are again indicative of pathology within the professional consciousness of ministers. They do not know who they are; therefore they do not know what role to play. The problem cannot be solved by playing a role, but only through that Spirit that informs any role. When we are primarily concerned with being ministers to persons and see any role only as a means to this end, we are putting Spirit and form in their proper relationship. Jesus had a real problem with the "role players" of his day, but he knew that regardless of the particular role in which daily events cast him, his task was to reveal the redemptive love of God to human beings. Even such an obviously "religious" discussion as worship soon got down to the deep needs of the man or woman to whom he was speaking. On one occasion he did such an unorthodox thing as calling down out of a tree a man who seemed to show more anxious need than those on the ground. Pastors who are clear on the matter of the inner spirit and purpose of their ministry have no problem with role.

Jesus was inwardly free for a redemptive ministry to persons. This was all that counted. This he saw as the fulfillment of the law and the prophets, but he opposed applications of the law when they interfered with the needs of persons. If persons were hungry or needed to be healed, he broke the law in regard to the Sabbath. To him, helping people was far more important than any status symbol. He mingled with publicans and sinners, he forgave harlots, and he discussed with Nicodemus the need to be reborn. His reach into the life that opened itself to him was deeper than any human manifestation of estrangement, and he died forgiving those who closed their hearts to him. Here was a man who could truly love the unlovable. This was the ministry of reconciliation, and it is to this ministry that the pastor is called. But to meet people in a redemptive love that places human values above all other values demands an inner freedom. It is difficult to come into the possession of such freedom.

At great cost to himself, Jesus gained freedom for a redemptive ministry even to those who hated and killed him. Whatever the depth of suffering out of which human bitterness and estrangement grow, Jesus plumbed that depth. He could express the utter isolation of suffering by the words, "My God, my God, why hast thou forsaken me?" Following this, he could experience a reunion with God in faith, and he could say, "Into thy hands I commit my spirit." The meaning of pastoral care is that we must be able to enter into and suffer with those whom we seek to help. If our concern to help others ends with those who require little cost on our own part, then we will not help many. As genuine pastors we come to our people as ones who have taken their burden on ourselves, their suffering into ourselves. Not that we relieve them of their suffering, but in suffering with them and for them in love, we make it possible for them to find the redemptive answer in love. The preaching of the Word of the Cross is but a futile gesture unless we are able to manifest that Word by taking suffering into ourselves. This means the ability to enter into deep empathy with others, feeling their pain, their anxiety, guilt and hate, but maintaining the integrity of the self in trust and love.

In the ministry of Jesus we see complete freedom from the human tendencies to exploit and manipulate. He was open and transparent before all, and therefore he could help people see themselves and what they were becoming and what they might become. Such openness is frightening to some, and the frightened ones became Jesus' enemies because they saw that he would destroy in them what they were not ready to give up. His accessibility seemed to invite his friends to manipulate him into fulfilling their own image of him. This was the problem of Peter; but in Peter manipulativeness was finally mastered by a deeper and saving reality. The identity of Jesus was as a Servant of God, a suffering Servant who was to live out his mission concretely in the service of others, reaching into the depths of human need and remaining personally and spiritually available. This is also an identity in which modern pastors will find strength for ministry.

Finally, this ministry is not *our* ministry, but the continuation of Christ's ministry in us through his Spirit. The motive force of the pastoral ministry should not be our own problems or needs, although it is very difficult to eliminate these completely. The temptation in the ministry to work out various ego needs, to find disguised expression of sexual or hostile impulses, to project our own anxieties and guilts onto others, is very subtle, extensive, and potent. It is particularly dangerous because it operates unconsciously. There are strong forces at work within the personalities of pastors, as well as the persons to whom they minister, to keep certain needs out of awareness.

One way for pastors to deal with this problem in themselves is through the constant reminder that ministry is not their private affair but is the ministry of Christ through them. Constant self-examination in the light of the Spirit of Christ as revealed in the Gospels, in relation to the specific persons to whom pastors minister, should be a source of insight and growth. To meet another person in the name of Christ is not a merely formal relationship, nor is it a role to be played. "Inasmuch as you have done it unto one of the least of these, you have done it unto me" has profound spiritual implications for the pastoral ministry. The model for Christian ministers is not a formal one that we can imitate or follow to the letter. It is a living model of the Spirit, and this is the Spirit of Christ. It is in this Spirit that true pastors fulfill their calling.

NOTES

1. See James D. Smart, *The Rebirth of the Ministry* (Philadelphia: Westminster Press, 1960).

2. Seward Hiltner, *Preface to Pastoral Theology* (New York: Abingdon Press, 1958).

3. Richard Niebuhr, *The Purpose of the Church and Its Ministry* (New York: Harper & Row, 1956).

4. Samuel W. Blizzard, "The Parish Minister's Self-Image of His Master Role," in *Pastoral Psychology,* December 1958, and also "The Parish Minister's Self-Image and Variability in Community Culture," in *Pastoral Psychology,* October 1959.

≺ **2** ≻

The Meaning of Pastoral Care

PASTORAL CARE IS THE ART of communicating the inner meaning of the gospel to persons at the point of their need. Thus pastoral care is not a theoretical discipline, although it may be undergirded by such disciplines as theology or biblical interpretation. Pastoral care is not "pastoral theology," especially when this term denotes a set of principles for the conduct of a specific activity. Pastoral care is more a function than an activity, more a living relationship than a theory or interpretation, more a matter of being than of doing. It is the manifestation in the relationship between pastor and persons, either individually or in groups, of a quality of life that points to, and gives a basis in experience for, the realization of the love of God. The love of the pastor is not to be identified with the love of God, in that the pastor is weak, imperfect, and finite. But the pastor can be "with" a person in a manner that gives reality and meaning to the infinite love of God, or the pastor may block the realization of that meaning. In a sense, any genuine human love is the manifestation of the love of God, since it is the gift of God shed abroad in our hearts through the Holy Spirit.

In the term "pastoral care" the word "care" expresses concern, and the word "pastoral" gives depth and direction to that concern. Thus pastoral care is distinctly different from "medical care." We have indicated that the pastor's concern is rooted in the gospel. As Christians we are called to love others as God in Christ has loved us. As Christian pastors we have special duties and responsibilities, and we should have specialized training to

8

qualify us for our work. In addition, we need experiences that will develop our capacities for self-giving love.

Although the gospel is the beginning and end of the pastoral ministry, pastors must also be concerned with the human factors that control or influence a person's perception of, and responses to, that gospel. No human being receives and responds to the gospel, either for the first time or after long experience within the church, with pristine eyes and soul. We rather receive it against a background of ideas, feelings, and personality structures that predispose us to accept, reject, or distort the image and interpretation of Christ as found in the New Testament. These predisposing elements grow out of our experiences with other human beings in our family and in cultural relationships, and out of our responses to these relationships. These statements will receive some elaboration later. Here we must stress the principle that genuine pastors are not satisfied to blame the rejection and distortion of the gospel on the generalized idea of sin. They are concerned with the specific processes within the individual that give rise to attitudes, and they understand that at least some of the effects of destructive experiences and relationships can be overcome by creative and redemptive relationships and processes. Genuine pastors see themselves as a medium of healing rather than of condemnation.

What Is the Communication of the Gospel?

We have defined pastoral care as the communication of the gospel to persons at the point of their need. Two obvious questions arise in any discussion of this concept. What is the gospel that is to be communicated? And how is it communicated? Effective communication can take place only through means that can embody the reality to be communicated.

What is the gospel? A full discussion of the content of the gospel is obviously impossible here. Christian pastors must have a thorough biblical, theological, and historical training through which the elaboration of this question will take place. We are interested here in the nature of the gospel as it bears on the kind of communication that is required in pastoral care.

The gospel is usually described as the good news of God's redeeming love as revealed in Jesus Christ. The modern mind,

saturated with the latest televised news reports, is likely to identify the gospel with something that can be communicated by
verbal and mechanical means. But the reality of the gospel is
something deeper than this. As Alan Richardson says, "After the
death and resurrection of Jesus the content of the Gospel, as it
is understood by the Apostolic Church, is Christ himself."[1] The
gospel, then, is a Person, and through this Person, a living relationship with God. The gospel was embodied in a Person whose
relationships with human beings have been taken to reveal the
redemptive, reconciling relationship that God offers to all. In
Jesus, God has taken the initiative in offering and demonstrat-
ing this relationship, and in Jesus the relationship was accepted
and lived out. As human beings have responded, and still respond, in love and faith to Christ, we experience redemption or
reconciliation with God. We are no longer separated and alien-
ated and therefore lost. We experience the inner reality of God's
acceptance of us as sons and daughters. This new relationship
results in a new sense of being that enables us to move toward
discovering and becoming the persons we are potentially. The
suffering of Christ speaks of an aspect of the nature of God that
reaches out to us on the level of our own deepest suffering, the
anxiety caused by alienation from God. The gospel is Christ
himself and the power of the new relationship that God has offered to humankind through Christ.

This emphasis on the gospel as a living relationship embodied in the person and work of Christ is pointedly expressed in
the New Testament. The Pauline statement, "God was in Christ
reconciling the world unto himself" (2 Cor. 5:19), is one expression, and another is to be found in the Johannine phrase, "The
Word became flesh and dwelt among us" (John 1:14). God's
message to humankind concerning God's redemptive love may
be put into words, but the deepest and only fully adequate means
of communication of God's love to human beings was its incarnation in a Person and its expression in the relationship of that
Person with other persons in a historical setting. The idea of
the Incarnation is not only a means of interpreting the meaning
of Christ, but it also describes God's most effective means of
communication with human beings. It is a demonstration in
depth, a communication through Being, on a level far deeper
than the verbal. Christ is indeed the "Word of God," but of-

ten we slip unconsciously into the human error of confusing our words about Christ with the reality of Christ himself. Also, it is not easy verbalisms about the gospel, but the Spirit of Christ incarnate in a human being that is the deepest and most effective form of communication of the gospel today. This level of communication is the core of pastoral care, and should find expression through all the activities of the pastor.

The principle of communication involved in our concept of pastoral care is simply that the nature of any reality determines the way in which it can be communicated. Mathematical reality is such that is can be communicated through impersonal symbols. On the other hand, the redemptive reality that is God's love is deeply personal. It comes to each of us in terms of our own existence and our own problems. It concerns each person's being as we are related to Ultimate Being. We suffer because of a broken relationship in our personal existence. We find healing through a person who calls us back into a very personal unity of purpose and meaning, who addresses us as a person, a Thou rather than an It. People may speak to us with their lips and reach only the surface of our being, our conscious, intellectual processes. The deeper level of being is reached only through what people are to us, and through our response of openness and trust to them as persons. God in Christ is made known to us in the struggles of our being and becoming — Person to person, Spirit to spirit. The pastor may proclaim the love of God verbally, but the reality of this love is not communicated unless the pastor enters in love and understanding, in the power of the Spirit of God, into the sufferings and estrangement of the individual person. Even in preaching to a large congregation, real communication does not take place until something behind and beyond the words of the preacher finds a positive response in the very being of a hearer so that a process of growth or healing is begun.

There is an incident in the life of Jesus that brings particular reinforcement to our interpretation. It is when Jesus is accused of casting out demons by the power of Beelzebub (Luke 11:14–23). After pointing out that a kingdom divided against itself cannot stand, Jesus goes on to say, "But if it is by the finger of God that I cast out demons, then the kingdom of God has come upon you." In other words, the very process of healing a man of a demon is in itself a proclamation of the Kingdom of God. In such healing something profound occurred between Jesus and the sick man, something that those about him could not observe. Only the results could be seen, but they could not be believed. The observers were frightened because the results bore witness to something beyond their understanding and they could not accept a deeper insight. Therefore it must be evil. But Jesus emphasized that the Kingdom of God became real in the very presence of himself with the possessed man, and in the healing that resulted.

Many pastors have a too limited and frightened view of their significance as pastors, and this seriously limits their effectiveness. They are more concerned with "not going too far" than they are in discovering the healing of self-giving, suffering love. In the very act of healing and of promoting growth, whether it be the healing of the fear of a little child, the guilt of an adolescent, or the sense of futility and meaninglessness in an adult, the Kingdom of God may be proclaimed and realized more surely than by most preachers from the pulpit. In the quality of loving relationships that meet the daily spiritual needs of persons so that growth becomes possible, the Kingdom is also proclaimed through demonstration. Pastoral care is not an adjunct to the ministry; it is the very core.

The early church distinguished between two kinds of verbal communication, the kerygma and the didache. The first was the central proclamation of the church, the work of God in Christ, particularly as revealed in the Cross and the Resurrection. The didache was the ethical teaching that followed upon the acceptance of the gospel message. However, it is difficult to read the pages of the New Testament, particularly the Gospels, and not discover a third and deeper level of communication. The kerygma and didache formulate, structuralize, and elaborate in concepts the relationship that God offers human beings. But this living relationship in which deep reconciliation is experienced can never be known or communicated through verbal formulation alone. It was known to the first Christians through the Person of Jesus; when it is known in successive generations it is through persons who are able to manifest it on a nonverbal level. This is the difference between a theological statement on pastoral care and pastoral care as a living relationship in which

a healing love is manifest. In the New Testament this is understood as the work of the Holy Spirit, the Spirit of God in Christ,
reaching out to the human spirit. The pastor is called to continue the work of Christ by loving others in a finite way and
thus pointing to the redemptive love of God.

The concept of pastoral care as developed here moves beyond any theology that is proclaimed only verbally. It returns
to a historical Jesus revealed in the Gospels, a Person authenti-
cating his words by his life, by what others experienced him to
be. He spoke with authority, not as one leaning on authorities.
Of him it was written: "We have beheld his glory, glory as of
the only Son from the Father" (John 1:14). And again, "From
his fullness have we all received, grace upon grace" (John 1:16).
Such interpretations of the Person of Jesus are grounded in the
power and grace that others felt in him as they were able to open
their lives to him in trust.

Theological scholarship offers some support at this point.
Paul Althaus quotes Gunther Bornkamm's remark concerning
Bultmann's position: "Jesus has become a mere fact of salva-
tion, and is no longer a person."[2] Althaus goes on to say,

> The fact that the person of Jesus as such (of whose con-
> crete characteristics we can, in Bultmann's words, "now
> know practically nothing") has no place in the *kerygma,*
> leads to serious theological consequences. The power of
> the Gospel to overcome our unbelief depends on the fact
> that the *kerygma* includes the gospels with their concrete
> picture of Jesus. In the picture of the man Jesus we lay
> hold of the character of God, in the spiritual countenance
> of Jesus we behold the countenance of God. The living
> eyes of a man look at us out of the gospels and compel our
> faith. The *kerygma* is a statement, a dogma, if we do not
> see it filled out by the living picture of Jesus as the gospels
> portray Him.

And we are suggesting that in genuine pastoral care there is an
additional factor, a nonverbal expression of the meaning of the
gospel through the relationship of pastor and person.

Pastoral experience, as well as the gospel itself, clearly indicates the necessity of the mutual involvement of pastor and

person. In this involvement the pastor is not just another person — a father, a mother, a friend — but is one whose involvement demonstrates and gives living substance to the message of God's grace. Effective pastoral care, that is, meeting a person at the point of need, demands that pastors become involved in the very existence and predicament of other persons, their tensions, sufferings, meanings, values, joys. This involvement can take place only through a deeply empathic experience. Pastors cannot stand off and observe in detachment. We should not assume a relationship of control, manipulation, or domination toward others, nor should we permit others to exercise these attitudes over us. Pastoral involvement, sometimes called identification, requires that pastors be their genuine selves to others, and not put on a front. We must seek to understand how others feel by honestly admitting to ourselves how we would feel in a similar situation. We must seek to understand the needs, goals, and purposes of others, taking seriously their value system and the meaning they attach to experience. This identification is never complete — pastors must always maintain a clear sense of their own identity as distinct from that of another.

Such involvement requires participation with others in their experience, rather than doing things for others or to them. It requires a genuine self-giving love, an inner freedom to do or be what is necessary to help another find full self-realization. In such involvement pastors are concerned to help others find their own answers, and pastors need to be very sensitive to understand and control any tendency in themselves to become part of the answer. Pastors also identify with the gospel, with Christ in whose name they work, and with the church, but these identifications should strengthen pastors to identify with those for whom Christ died.

This involvement, grounded in identification and empathy, is not possible by following directions. It depends upon the level of emotional maturity of the pastor. If pastors are emotionally immature, they will develop immature relationships with their people, without knowing that they are doing so. Various characteristics of immaturity, such as dependence, passivity, and manipulation and control of others, will be manifest in the relationship of emotionally immature pastors. More mature persons will sense such qualities and will avoid deep relationships with them. Genuine pastors must maintain their own integrity at all times; otherwise they will be able to help no one.

Such empathic involvement is not easily accepted by all persons in our culture. Indeed, one source of problems is the inability of some persons to open themselves to another. Absolute trustworthiness is an essential quality in the helper. Pastors must be the kind of persons who can be so trusted that others will invite them to share the realities of their existence, especially those that are painful, in which they have already been hurt. Such trust and openness can come to pastors, not because they have any particular brand of theology, but because they are genuinely loving, trustworthy persons. Pastors also must have the wisdom to know what really helps and what does harm in various human situations. But pastors should not expect that everyone will respond to them favorably.

The involvement of the pastor in the pastoral relationship is not just as another person, although the personal dimension of the life of the pastor is never eliminated, but is primarily as a servant to God, bringing a ministry of redemptive love. While many professions "do something" for others, the task of the pastor is not so much in the realm of doing as of being. It is a matter of being the kind of person who helps others find their own true relationship to God, that inwardly they may become whatever in the grace of God they can become, and at the same time function adequately in relation to themselves and to others.

Communication on this level has the quality of revelation. It is always a two-way process; there can be no understanding of others unless we are able to reveal ourselves. In pastoral relationships, persons generally wait for pastors to reveal themselves, and their self-revelation is governed by the quality of what the pastors reveal about themselves. Any response to another person is a form of self-revelation; to respond is to reveal something about oneself. The response may reveal defensiveness or openness, fear or courage, or any other personal quality. God becomes known to human beings through God's own self-revelation.

We constantly see in the counseling experience that for persons to reveal themselves to another is also to make a self-discovery. Indeed, an essential element in the therapeutic process is that of helping persons find "insight," i.e., self-discovery, by actually experiencing themselves in the presence of someone who knows how to accept and understand their revelation. Such communication is not primarily a matter of words, although words are involved. But deeper feelings and strivings must be revealed. The Christian doctrine of revelation has profound implications for pastoral care if we see revelation as a process that is continually deepening our relationships, by which we become known to each other and to ourselves in a mutual relationship before God. Many of us cannot understand and accept the revelation of God because our discovery and revelation of ourselves has been blocked.

The futility of communication in which there is no deep involvement, no revelation and self-discovery, is illustrated by the following editorial from the *Chicago Daily News,* January 27, 1964:

NO PLACE FOR JERRY HOLLINS

Ours is a big, rich, exciting city; its shops are bulging with goods, its streets full of shiny cars; its theaters and restaurants full of well-to-do people.

And there is Jerry Hollins.

Jerry Hollins was born in Louisiana, and lived there for 25 years.

But there is not much future for a young man in Louisiana if he is a Negro; and the word keeps coming down about how good things are up North, especially in Chicago.

Two years ago Jerry Hollins came to Chicago to look for work. He didn't find much, and when he found it, it didn't last long.

Recently he took to hanging around the Greyhound bus station, and when a policeman asked him why he was loitering there, and he didn't have a good reason, he was arrested for disorderly conduct.

The judge set his fine at $100. Hollins didn't have $100. He didn't have anything.

In the House of Correction he worked out the fine in the laundry. Nobody came to see him, and he listed no relatives.

At 9 a.m. Thursday he was let out of the House of Correction, and at 1:30 p.m. he crawled out on a ledge in the U.S. Court House rotunda, seven stories above the lobby floor.

It took him so long to work up his nerve that firemen were able to get there with a net, and when he jumped, they caught him and broke his fall. He suffered a broken pelvis, a collapsed lung, broken ribs, and other serious injuries.

Just before Hollins jumped a minister caught his attention. "God loves you," the minister said.

Hollins asked, "What God?"

Nobody seems to have given Jerry Hollins an answer.

This points to what is wrong with so much pastoral care — it stands back at a safe distance and verbalizes a message. There is no involvement with persons, no revelation and self-discovery, and no discovery of God. "What God?" is a question that can be answered only in a relationship in which revelation and discovery are simultaneous experiences.

The kind of involvement of which we have been speaking is characteristic of the relationship that Jesus had with those he met. In the words of James D. Smart:

> Jesus' pastoral relationship with his disciples and with others was one in which he laid himself open to them in an unconditional way, interpenetrated their situation with his love and understanding, and took upon himself the burden of their sins, distresses, and anxieties. He gave himself to them, not in any sentimental way, but in the profoundest identification of himself with them. He made himself one with them, so that they were conscious of his not judging them from without but understanding them from within.[3]

This view of pastoral care seems to be in conflict with certain theological views, particularly the doctrine of the "sovereignty of grace." Before we examine this doctrine specifically, a few words are necessary in regard to the relation of doctrine in general to human experience.

Pastors deal primarily with persons, not with ideas or doctrines. In this way we may differ radically from many theologians who are absorbed in ideas and are only theoretically concerned with persons — although we must recognize that this is not true of all theologians. However, pastors need to avoid the temptation of finding security in ideas to such an extent that they put themselves in something of an intellectual and operational strait jacket. When this occurs in pastors, they will seek to put others in the same doctrinal framework.

The weakness of an approach that is primarily doctrinal is that the dynamic processes of human life cannot be controlled and manipulated or placed in a strait jacket without hurting persons. There is an element of spontaneity in human experience and a drive toward autonomy and self-determination that is either crushed by a too rigid doctrinal approach or that may motivate a person to rebel and reject the whole of the Christian faith. On the other hand, it has been frequently remarked that people may seek the security of doctrine in order to avoid the heavy responsibility of autonomy. There are indications that this has taken place in recent years in the field of pastoral care and counseling.

An intellectual system can begin with a certain premise, and from there be developed by rejecting all contradictory ideas. But life itself cannot be confined to any system, since it is dynamic, always in motion, opening from within, or else deteriorating. Persons are not machines and are not completely predictable in any logical or mathematical manner. Intellectual formulations may serve the purposes of life, but life should not be asked to serve the purposes of the formulations, that is, to stay within them. No finite mind has yet produced the infallible and completely comprehensive intellectual system. Systems therefore must be kept flexible — growing and changing with each new insight from life. This is particularly true for pastors, who are dealing with the profound level of the life of the spirit, which least of all is subject to human systems of operation. Perhaps this accounts for the fact that the work of the Holy Spirit has been so neglected — the Holy Spirit cannot be restricted to human intellectual formulations.

The doctrine of the sovereignty and sufficiency of grace, coming down from the Reformers, is a good example of a religious insight that can be used in either a creative or a restrictive way. An illustration of its restrictive use is cited by George Hendry in discussing the Reformers. He says,

> The sufficiency of grace alone left no need of correlation with anything on the part of man, but implied rather his total incapacity.... The Reformers rapidly lost interest in the human spirit altogether and for an obvious reason: When the full force of their new apprehension of the Gospel was deployed theologically, it seemed to obliterate the spirit of man and reduce them to the level of an inanimate object like a stone or tree.[4]

Or in the words of Calvin, "Man is so enslaved by sin as to be of his own nature incapable of an effort, or even an aspiration, toward that which is good."[5]

Hendry presents philosophical, biblical, and theological objections to this view of the sovereignty and sufficiency of grace, and we shall not summarize these here. We are more concerned at the moment to distinguish between two aspects of the problem particularly relevant to pastors. Pastors, from the perspective of Christian commitment, understand the ultimate nature of God and the finite nature of human beings. God in God's ultimate nature is in no way dependent upon human beings. But God, as manifest to human beings, has made the divine self dependent on human response, or else human beings are automata, puppets, and not free spirits. That human beings have no power within themselves to do some things for themselves is belied by many creative experiences in pastoral care, even with those who are in a state of profound mental illness. That we do this in relationship, not by ourselves, is also indisputably evidenced in pastoral care. That we have the ability to learn to control our own response to what is given us on a human level cannot be doubted. That we have the power to determine our response to God is unquestionable. In God's gracious approach to human beings, God does not take over and force us to make a favorable response.

One of the essentials of the pastor is a working understanding of the role of Creation in human life. To assume that our freedom and ability to arrive at decisions involving our own destiny are of our own making is false. Human beings are what we are in part through certain gifts and graces bestowed upon us in the act of Creation. If we have freedom, it was given to us as a gracious act of God, the Creator. We do not create our own freedom, but we participate actively in its realization. This is at least part of the meaning of the insight that human beings were made in the image of God. The gracious redemptive activity of God in Jesus Christ is directed toward the human beings whom God has already created. But redemption is not forced on us; our cooperation is essential. Creation and redemption are thus two sides of the same coin; the power that we have to do something for ourselves is not of our own making but is a gift of God's Creation. And it never comes to its fruition in isolation, but always in relationship to others. This is the essential truth in the idea of the sufficiency of grace. Grace is given in relationships.

John Wesley's concept of prevenient grace lies closer to the heart of pastoral experience. He says,

> There is no man that is in a state of mere nature; there is no man, unless he has quenched the Spirit, that is wholly void of the grace of God. No man living is entirely destitute of what is vulgarly called *natural conscience.* But this is not natural; it is more properly termed, *preventing grace.* Every man has a greater or less measure of this, which waiteth not for the call of man. Every man has, sooner or later, good desires, although the generality of men stifle them before they can strike deep roots, or produce any considerable fruit.... So that no man sins because he has not grace, but because he does not use the grace which he hath.[6]

In pastoral care is it not enough to tell people that grace is available for them, but rather one must be to them a person through whom a measure of grace — often in terms of strength, courage, and hope — is experienced. When counselors consider the amount of strength available within a troubled person, we are thinking in terms of prevenient grace, whether we use these words or not.

The heart of our problem lies in human nature. We live

and move and have our being in an ultimate Creator-Redeemer God. God's redemptive process continues human creation and perfects it. But human existence is on a finite level, and human beings have had difficulty in handling the tensions that arise out of the conflict between the demands and meanings of an ultimate, final relationship, and the more immediate, finite aspects of human nature and existence. Scholars have formulated this problem in various ways. Tillich's formulation of the problem of salvation in terms of existentialism is well known.[7] Thornton, following Bonhoeffer, uses the terms "ultimate" and "penultimate" in wrestling with the problem.[8] Whatever terms pastors use to formulate the problem and the answers, they need to understand the operational dynamics involved in persons. By this we mean that experiences on the proximate level of life, particularly in human relationships, are a determining factor in the individual's perception of, and response to, God and Christ. Much rebellion against God is really rebellion against human parents. Helpful pastors will seek to assist such persons to gain insight into, and work through, the destructive feelings developed on the human level as a means of resolving problems in their relationship or response to God. For this reason, verbal formulation is not sufficient, although when skillfully used it may prove helpful. Verbal formulation of religious meaning does not change the dynamic factors in an individual's perception and response. Many persons are so absorbed with the problems and difficulties on the proximate, existential level of life, and their powers of response are so dulled by both external and inner pressures, that they are unable to be concerned with ultimate meanings. To condemn them as sinners, or even to describe them in such terms, may mean that the pastoral concern is without redemptive purpose. The pastor must be concerned to alleviate the conditions, external and internal, that underlie their spiritual lethargy.

One illustration will suffice. Recently a student came to an interview after a class period in which Christian love had been discussed. One point stressed by the teacher was that Christian love involves the sharing of oneself with others. The student felt drawn to the idea and could see its applicability in his own life. Sharing himself with others was just what he could not do. He had built a shell around himself, and he found it very difficult to open himself to others. He had recently opened himself to another student in what seemed to be a friendship, but which developed quickly in dimensions that created intense guilt and frustration. So he had withdrawn again, and was more afraid than ever to open himself to anyone. The result of the class was an intense sense of guilt and frustration. He had received a verbal communication that he could see was directly related to his own experience. The communication did not create the problem, but merely put it into words and intensified his awareness. But his thinking led to dead ends: the problem remained, "How do I get to the point where I can overcome my fear and open myself to others?" He could talk about the problem in its Christian theological dimensions, but this only brought on a deeper level of anxiety as he saw himself unable to be what he thought God wanted him to be. The confrontation with himself in terms of basic attitudes was very deep. In terms of understanding the roots of those attitudes and of working them out so that they no longer controlled him, nothing had yet been accomplished. The accomplishment of this was a real work of pastoral care, requiring a long relationship with a person of genuine love, understanding, and skill to help him overcome his fear and respond in trust. He had to have help with problems on the human level primarily within himself before the ultimate relationships could be resolved. The meaning for God's love of him had to be mediated through a person in order for it to become his own experience; this could not be made to happen by verbalization alone.

The idea of the sovereignty and sufficiency of grace must be balanced, as it is in the New Testament and in life, by human freedom and responsibility on the level of the proximate, the human aspects of life. That human beings have no power to control or manipulate God should be obvious. That God has not made human beings to be automata, puppets, seems evident. Our response to the grace of God is controlled within us. We are always in tension because there is a power working within us that is not of our own making, yet as far as our individual existence is concerned, we have freedom and responsibility of decision. We must also experience the consequences of our decision within ourselves.

And there is another source of our tension. Our freedom and

autonomy are threatened by the fact that there is much in our existence that determines the manner in which our freedom is used. The drive toward autonomy begins to express itself early in life, but it may be thwarted and denied by anxious parents. Relationships with humans may be such that individuals gradually lose their power of autonomy as they mature. This means that they will become sick, that is, unable to function as human beings. If the sickness is extreme, people are relieved from all human responsibility and decisions are made for them. Recovery or cure may require a long relationship with a genuinely loving and understanding person.[9] But the avoidance of such a tragedy in the first place also requires a relationship of love and understanding within a framework of constructive values in the entire process of growing up.

Truly creative pastoral care takes into account the various dimensions of human life and gives them adequate consideration. A one-sided emphasis on either the experience of grace or that of freedom or on the determining influences in human life leads to a distorted approach. Theological ideas such as the complete impotence of human beings may express the power of guilt to produce self-depreciation. On the other hand, an overemphasis on human powers to save ourselves apart from a living relationship with God may express human pride and defensiveness. Pastors will need to understand theological ideas not only according to their theological meaning, but also in terms of the way in which they are used defensively by persons.

The question of God's power to work directly in human life is usually raised at this point. That God has the power to do this is not in question. The question is whether God does enter human life and take over against our will. Are there times when God rescinds our freedom and forces us into some particular behavior? Or are all of God's relationships with human beings characterized by grace that permits a free response, even rejection?

The question of God's working directly in human life, that is, operating apart from human freedom, needs examination from another angle. Pastors are likely to find some persons who are sure this has happened to them. Sometimes — not always — these folks are found in mental hospitals. They are the victims of a psychotic condition in which contents from their own unconscious are identified as the voice or action of God. There is much compulsiveness in such experience, that is, such individuals do feel compelled to think or act in certain ways and may believe that God is forcing them to do this. In milder forms, this same experience may occur in almost any religious community. These experiences convey a deep sense of the mysterious, and we must not permit ourselves to be misled by this. While we should not openly dispute the person's interpretation, we must also avoid agreeing with that interpretation and thus confirming the illness.

That God does work in human life is a deep conviction of the Christian faith. There is a sense in which our entire existence is created and sustained by the love and power of God. This is part of the meaning of the doctrine of Creation and of Wesley's concept of prevenient grace. But on the level of conscious awareness, God works through a gracious, loving relationship in which the cooperation of the human agent is an active component. Prayer and worship are experiences in which such conscious awareness and cooperation can develop on the part of human beings; or they may be used for the opposite result. God does work in human life, but in a way that does not rob us of the basic meaning of "personhood," the power of autonomous decision within the framework of responsibility.

Human beings, then, are finite creatures who have the capacity to experience meanings and relationships that are seen as being on the level of the ultimate. As finite creatures, we may know God, our creator. This is the crowning characteristic of personhood, the power to shape the immediate in terms of ultimate goals and purposes, to experience a personal relationship with God. God's self-revelation in Christ was communication in personal relationship. Insight into ultimate purposes, goals, and relationships must become operative on the levels of the immediate and the finite. Otherwise they will have no significance for the finite aspects of our lives, a situation that has frequently existed in religion. It is only as these two aspects of human life become dynamically related that we find our fulfillment.

Since pastoral care is primarily communication on the level of relationships, the incarnational principle must be operative in all the pastor's relationships. Otherwise, pastors may speak the words of the faith without communicating the reality of the faith. This in no way limits the sovereignty and sufficiency of grace; it only describes the basis on which that grace becomes real. And unless that grace does become real in the immediate or proximate levels of life, unless it has something to bring to persons as they undergo the joys, conflicts, and suffering of life, religion becomes only a sick fantasy about the next world. We already have too much of this.

The principle of the Incarnation not only involves the pastor, but the entire Christian community. From the earliest days of the Hebrew-Christian faith, God chose to work through the faithful community. The fact that this community was not always faithful did not destroy the purposes of God, but it did interfere with their fruition. Where a living church is brought into existence, there God works in and through the human community. Some churches are so dead spiritually that it is no wonder that persons brought up in them do not understand this truth. They cannot understand what they have not experienced.

On the level of spirit the only method of communication of reality is through experience. All people need a priest, and all who would grow into the Christian faith need a community in which grace is manifest — not because of God's inadequacy, but because of our inability to comprehend what we have not experienced. Some of the importance of the doctrine of the priesthood of all believers lies in the fact that before we can honestly open ourselves to God, we may first need to learn to open ourselves to one who stands in the place of God. If we have not known love on the human level we cannot comprehend the meaning of the love of God. We will respond to the verbal message of the love of God in terms of infantile fantasy grounded in deprivation, a fantasy of infantile magic, and our religious experience will be highly emotional with no deep volitional content. Or we will reject the idea of God's love because we are unable to experience any sense of inner reality in it. Or we may struggle to accept the idea of God's love without any deep sense of reality or meaning. Love becomes real only through loving relationships, not through words about love.

It may be objected that this interpretation will encourage the pastor to "play God." This brings up one of the professional hazards of the ministry. Such problems grow from two sources. One is the sense of inferiority in pastors against which we react with ideas of being superior persons. The other is the very responsibility that pastors fulfill as preachers and priests. This places pastors in the position of persons who are standing in the place of God and speaking for God. The great professional temptation of pastors is to proceed gradually and unconsciously from the role as representatives of God to an unconscious fantasy of themselves as God. Then pastors begin to play God: to become authoritarian, dictatorial, dogmatic, punishing; to assert the superiority of their wisdom and theology; and to seek to overpower others from this position. We do not mean that these are the characteristics of God as God is seen in Christ. Certainly they are not. They are the characteristics that the human ego takes on when it tries to play God.

Understanding the meaning of their relationship to others and to God should help pastors avoid the temptation to "play God." For when pastors see themselves as mediators, that is, persons whose relationship may have meaning to others on two levels, the proximate and the ultimate, the human and the divine, pastors should be moved to humility. Indeed, if we understand Paul's interpretation of the incarnational experience correctly, it involved emptying oneself of pride. "Though he was in the form of God, [Jesus] did not count equality with God a thing to be grasped, but emptied himself, taking the form of a servant, being born in the likeness of men" (Phil. 2:1–11). It may be objected that this statement applies to Jesus but not to the rest of us, and in a special way this is true. But in another sense this interpretation is not limited to Jesus. Pastors must likewise "empty themselves" and take on the "form of a servant," accepting their human existence as that through which God can work for God's own glory and for the reconciliation of human beings to God. God is not an authoritarian director or a supermanipulator of our will, but One who is revealed by a sharing of human suffering in self-giving love on the Cross. God's ministers, if they are to bring to people the reality of this love, have no other way but through self-giving love in which human pride in intellect or power is transformed into suffering love. The genuine pastoral relationship is an experience in humility.

The pastor, then, is one through whom the love of God is made real in human relationships in which the pastor's love speaks of the greater love of God. In suggesting that the pastor is something of a mediator, we are well aware that the New Testament speaks of the "one mediator between God and man, the man Christ Jesus" (1 Tim. 2:5). Accepting the uniqueness of the mediatory work of Christ, we must go on to emphasize again that Jesus himself indicated to his disciples that they were to carry on his work in his Spirit, and through power which would be given to them as they needed. As Luther put it, our task is to be as "little Christs to our neighbors."[10] Or as a modern theologian puts it, "Because the grace of God portrayed itself perfectly in Christ, it can portray itself imperfectly in others."[11] It is indeed a miracle that God's grace can enter human experience through the imperfect love of another human being and still make itself known in its fullness. Such mediation is grounded in the divine initiative through Creation and redemption; it promotes rather than interferes with communion with God; it places the pastor in a living relationship with God and others, that is, we are to love those whom we serve just as God in Christ has loved both us and them. We would not confine this level of communication to the pastor. It is also the responsibility of the laity. But we are saying that it is this dimension that distinguishes real pastoral care from mere pastoral activity. The pastor should have a level of training and wisdom in such matters beyond that which most laypersons are privileged to acquire.

Pastoral Care and the Holy Spirit

In stressing the place of relationships in the communication of the gospel, and the incarnational nature of genuine Christian relationships, we are obviously approaching what has been called the extension of the Incarnation. Christian thought has largely rejected this concept, probably in order to preserve the uniqueness of the Person of Christ. While this may be structurally and theologically sound, pastors, constantly dealing with the processes of life rather than with formulations about them, must keep their attention focused on what happens between persons and within persons in Christian experience. In Christian thought this means moving away from the concept of the extension of the Incarnation to that of the Holy Spirit. In the New

Testament the Holy Spirit is the gift of Christ to his disciples; it is the presence of Christ within the experience of his followers and "where two or three are gathered together." We therefore turn to a consideration of the relation of pastoral care to the work of the Holy Spirit.

There is a fundamental problem as to the meaning of human spirit and Holy Spirit, and of their relationship. It is not our intention to enter into this at any length.[12] However, pastoral care cannot accept a theological point of view that depreciates the human spirit or person. The pastor has many opportunities to observe the tremendous potential of the human spirit for growth and healing even under the most adverse conditions. We shall not attempt to draw a line between the activity of the human spirit and the Holy Spirit, for the Holy Spirit is manifest to human beings through a quality of relationship that makes such lines highly artificial and misleading. But the human spirit is completely passive only in those persons suffering from deeply neurotic passive dependence, and even here the potential for activity is present. To make such pathological conditions normative for the Christian faith is a mistake. The view that depreciates and devalues the human spirit is as deadly to creative pastoral care as is exclusive adherence to modern psychological determinism. Indeed, such adherence may represent refusal to accept the truly creative, spontaneous, and responsible aspects of the human spirit.

The concept of spirit needs to be taken out of the area of magic, ghosts, and goblins, and neither should it be used to explain in a vague way what we do not understand or to excuse ourselves from some kind of responsibility. Arnold B. Come in his *Human Spirit and Holy Spirit,* and following Kierkegaard, asserts that "man *qua* man ... is a realized indissolvable unity of body and soul, denoted by the term 'spirit,' or in contemporary language, 'self' or 'person.' Again he speaks of the 'I,' the self, the person, the spirit."[13] This places the manifestation of spirit exactly within the framework of personal relationships: the human person as spirit or self is called into being in relationship with other selves, and ultimately in relationship with God, the Supreme Self. God communicates to human beings through the manifestation of God's Spirit, through God's presence as a living Person in relationship with finite persons. In pastoral care, the spirit or self of the pastor, our presence or relationship with another person or persons, is a context through which the Holy Spirit may manifest itself.

The human spirit or self is weak when it experiences isolation or estrangement. Its growth and well-being require a relationship in which grace, in the form of love, support, and nurturance of others, is received. Such a relationship can take place on the human level. Human relationships always contain ambiguous elements, and in the relationship of the pastor there is the possibility of doing harm as well as good. No other quality of relationship, however, can fulfill the conditions that make it possible for another to respond in trust — the kind of trust that is essential for the development of the potentiality for autonomy. Thus the person who trusts must take a "leap of faith" in that we are never sure on the human level when a gracious person will become a hurtful one. Pastors need to become aware of the subtle ways in which they might hurt others. It is only the Holy Spirit that is free from such ambiguity and ambivalence.

But such experiences of grace are not for the selfish possession of the individual. The self that seeks to hold on to what it has been given will lose it. Grace is given that it may in turn be given again. It seems to be an unalterable law of life that as we have received, so do we give. The human spirit, or self, is enriched by gracious relationships with others, impoverished and deprived — as a result distorted — by relationships without meaning. In turn, the human spirit gives as it has received. As we have been loved, so we learn to love; as we have been accepted in grace, so are we able to accept others in grace. We give out of abundance of spirit, not out of poverty of spirit.

Dillistone describes the results of the activity of the Holy Spirit as life in unity, the gift of power, the establishment of order, and insight into the meaning and glory of God as seen in Jesus Christ.[14] The importance of these activities for pastoral care should be obvious. But it should also be evident that each of them is manifest in personal relationships. They are the manifestation of the presence of God with persons. In a partial sense they may be the result of the presence, or association, of one human being with another, depending on the nature of that association. Two words have been used in recent years to describe God's relation to human beings, and also to interpret the pastor's relation to others. They are both military words: "en-counter" and "confrontation." They grow out of experiences of armed conflict, where one side aggressively overcomes the other. The use of these warlike terms has evidently fulfilled a deep psychological need in many of our contemporaries. However, the biblical word for God's being with human beings is the one we have already used: "presence." It is a gracious presence, but for this very reason it may be disturbing and guilt-producing, calling us to responsibility and leading to decision. One has often heard young ministers talk about confronting others, and inevitably such talk is hostile and aggressive. These are hardly the means through which the gospel or the human aspects of the life of the spirit can be made real to others.

Rather, the communication of the gospel in pastoral care becomes effective through what Paul describes as the "fruits of the Spirit." He enumerates these as love, joy, peace, patience, kindness, goodness, faithfulness, gentleness, and self-control, qualities one might ascribe to the personality of Christ. When a person of these qualities associates with another in a significant relationship, something creative and redemptive may occur. But these qualities spring from the deep, interior levels of personality, within the self, or the spirit. They are called into being through a relationship in which they are manifested by the pastor, and they evoke from the recipient similar responses. They are qualities of the true human self in its fullest development. They are also the human side of God in Christ, that is, the qualities inspired by the Spirit of God in human life. They are the fruits of the Spirit and represent the deepest motivation of which a human being is capable. Pastors, in their relationships with others, will communicate these qualities insofar as they possess such qualities. They are not given once for all, but are constantly recreated, in part through communion with God and in part through human relationships.

There is another aspect of the work of the Holy Spirit in the communication of the gospel. The mediation of the fruits of the Spirit in human relationships strikes deep in the mind and spirit of the recipient. To feel oneself genuinely loved, accepted, and addressed as a person strikes deep chords of response. It may, under some conditions, such as in the men possessed by demons (Matt. 8:28–29), bring a response of intense fear and rejection. We have seen persons who, because of deep emotional and spiritual injuries, seemed completely incapable of making anything but a negative response to love or understanding. On the other hand, we have seen the opposite: the individual with a strong sense of having been rejected and unloved reaching out eagerly to grasp even a weak expression of love. The great helpers of humankind have been those who have been able to speak, sometimes in utter silence, to the deeper, creative levels of other persons.

It has been said that in psychotherapy the unconscious of the therapist speaks directly to the unconscious of the patient. In the words of a therapist, "the unconscious of the psychotherapist must move toward the unconscious longing of the patient and must promise the latter the fulfillment of that longing."[15]

This process is at work in pastoral care, even though it may not be recognized. It may be functioning between the preacher and some of the people in the pews, as well as in other pastoral relationships. It should be also recognized that in using such verbal symbols as God, Father, Christ, love, forgiveness, and in effectively communicating some of the spiritual reality for which these words stand, the pastor may be speaking more directly and effectively to the unconscious than does the therapist. Certainly much conscious meaning may be communicated through religious forms, and also the unconscious attitudes of the pastor are communicated without words. Putting this in theological terminology, we can say that spirit truly speaks to spirit, both through and without the use of words.

We turn now to one of Paul's interpretations of the work of the Spirit:

For the Spirit searches everything, even the depths of God. For what person knows a man's thoughts except the spirit of the man which is in him? So also no one comprehends the thoughts of God except the Spirit of God. Now we have received not the spirit of the world, but the Spirit which is from God, that we might understand the gifts bestowed on us by God. And we impart this in words not taught by human wisdom but taught by the Spirit, interpreting spiritual truths to those who possess the Spirit.

(1 Cor. 2:10–13)

We will try to understand this passage in the light of what we have been saying about verbal and nonverbal communication. The spirit of a person does know what is in that person, and it knows what it is seeking from others. The conscious self, however, in its weakness, may be seeking to conceal rather than to discover the truth about it. But even in this condition the person's own spirit may be restless, not wanting to face the pain of knowing but still searching for the answer to suffering. The drive toward cure may be operating even in persons with deep psychotic conditions. The spirit of a person does search the deepest thought, feelings, and motives of the person. And the Spirit of God does search everything, the depths of the person and the depths of God. When Christian pastors meet their people with some measure of the fruits of the Spirit, something creative may happen on a level deeper than consciousness. The Spirit of God, through the spirit of the pastor, may speak to a deep unconscious need and start a process of growth that eventually culminates in redemption. But this culmination must include the conscious self: that which was hidden must be brought to light and either accepted into the self or consciously modified or given up. A truly redemptive Christian experience requires conscious, responsible understanding and decisions. An experience in which the conscious self comes under the domination and control of unconscious impulses or feelings needs to be carefully scrutinized and worked through. But even then there are levels of human experience that are in the realm of mystery and can be only dimly apprehended, as through a glass darkly. One suspects that this passage from Paul contains part of his reflections on his own inner turmoil before and after the Damascus road experience, and that he is not able to express fully all that he feels or all that has happened to him, but that he is struggling to interpret it. One seems justified in suspecting that on the occasion of the stoning of Stephen (Acts 7:54–8:3), some powerful unconscious communication took place, and that the Spirit spoke through Stephen to a young man named Saul. The modern pastor needs to be as much a religious psychologist of the unconscious and a theologian of the Spirit as was Paul.

The Holy Spirit is the presence of Christ in human life. It is an experience that can be partly understood, yet it is also clothed in mystery. But its results may be seen in human life, in the fruits of the spirit. The best analogy for understanding the personal relationship of God with human beings is the personal relationship of person to person. A relationship between persons, or selves, on the human level, is the source of much of human glory and meaning — or of human destructiveness. But human relationships condition and predispose us to perceive and respond to the presence of Christ in like terms. Thus the demoniac (Matt. 8:28–29), possessed by an evil spirit, or self, begged Christ to depart from him. Pastors cannot manipulate or control the Holy Spirit. But their presence with a person, the quality of their spirit, may remove or create human obstacles to the work of the Holy Spirit. Pastors need to study their relationships, how they respond to others and how others respond to them. This area is to some extent within our own autonomous control and power to change.

In this chapter we have introduced the concept of pastoral care as the communication of the gospel to persons at the point of their need. We have stressed the inner reality of the relationship of God to human beings, and have asked how this is communicated. Verbal formulations communicate about this relationship. The reality of the relationship can be communicated only through experience. This has led to an incarnational theory of communication, and consequently of the work of the pastor. Or in terms of more traditional theology, it is the work of the Spirit, of the Holy Spirit present with the human spirit, bringing the human spirit, or self, to its fulfillment. For testimony of the incarnational aspect of communication of the gospel we go to a scholar in the field of missions, Eugene A. Nida, who in his book *Message and Mission* says,

All divine communication is essentially incarnational, for it comes not only in words, but in life. Even if a truth is given only in words, it has no real validity until it has been translated into life. Only then does the Word of life become life to the receptor. The words are in a sense nothing in and of themselves. . . . In the Incarnation of God in Jesus Christ, the Word (the expression and revelation of the wisdom of God) became flesh. This same fundamental principle has been followed throughout the history of the church, for God has constantly chosen to use not only words but human beings as well to witness to His grace; not only the message, but the messenger; not only the Bible, but the Church.[16]

NOTES

1. Alan Richardson, *A Theological Word Book of the Bible* (New York: Macmillan Company, 1951), p. 100.

2. Paul Althaus, *The So-Called Kerygma and the Historical Jesus,* trans. David Cairns (London: Oliver and Boyd, 1959), pp. 45–46.

3. James D. Smart, *The Rebirth of the Ministry* (Philadelphia: Westminster Press, 1960), p. 114.

4. George Hendry, *The Holy Spirit in Christian Theology* (Philadelphia: Westminster Press, 1956), p. 98.

5. Quoted in ibid., p. 99.

6. John Wesley, Sermon LXXXV, *Works* (London: John Mason, 1830), vol. 6, p. 512.

7. Paul Tillich, *Systematic Theology,* vol. 2 (Chicago: University of Chicago Press, 1957).

8. Edward Thornton, "Health and Salvation," in *The Journal of Religion and Health,* vol. 2, no. 3.

9. See Dorothy Baruch, *One Little Boy* (New York: Julian Press, 1952), and Gertrud Schwing, *A Way to the Soul of the Mentally Ill,* trans. Rudolph Ekstein and Bernard H. Hall (New York: International University Press, 1954).

10. Martin Luther, "Treatise on Christian Liberty," in *Collected Works* (Philadelphia: A.J. Holman Co., 1951), vol. 2, p. 338.

11. William Hordern, *A Layman's Guide to Protestant Theology* (New York: Macmillan Co., 1957).

12. See Hendry, *The Holy Spirit;* F. W. Dillistone, *The Holy Spirit in the Life of Today* (Philadelphia: Westminster Press, 1947); H. Wheeler Robinson, *The Christian Experience of the Holy Spirit* (New York: Harper & Row, 1928); Arnold B. Come, *Human Spirit and Holy Spirit* (Philadelphia: Westminster Press, 1959).

13. Come, *Human Spirit and Holy Spirit,* p. 37.

14. Dillistone, The Holy Spirit in the Life of Today.

15. Gertrud Schwing, A Way to the Soul of the Mentally Ill, p. 93.

16. Eugene A. Nida, *Message and Mission* (New York: Harper & Row, 1960), p. 226.

≺ **3** ≻

The Gospel for Persons:
Who Is a Person?

THE CONCEPT OF PASTORAL CARE that we have been developing is not analogous to a circle, which has a center; it is more like an ellipse, which has two foci. One focus is, of course, the gospel; the other is the person for whom the gospel is meant. In any ellipse there is always a dynamic tension between the two foci. In pastoral care the tension exists between the gospel and the person. Omit either of these foci, and pastoral care quickly becomes something else. This means that pastors must not only know and know about the gospel; they must also know and know about persons.

If we take a biblical approach to persons, we soon meet the question that was stated by the author of the eighth Psalm, "What is man that thou are mindful of him?" What is the human being? Christian theology has sought an answer to this question, and we need not elaborate its answer here. Human beings are made in the image of God, we are fallen sinners, we stand in need of the salvation that is from God in Christ. In these elements all people share and share alike. Individual experience is an expression of a universal truth.

But even as the Psalmist asks the question, the point of view shifts: "That thou are mindful of him,...and that thou dost care for him." This is a shift from an impersonal "what" to a personal "who." There is a shift from persons in the mass to the individual. The question now becomes "Who is this person?"

For when a relationship of caring is introduced, a human being ceases to be identified as one of a mass and stands out as a person. God as an I always addresses the person as a thou, not as an it or a thing. It is this personal relationship that calls an individual into being as a person.[1]

The experience of God's meeting an individual as a person is amply illustrated in the Bible. The revelation of Isaiah (chapter six) in the temple was an experience of the presence of God. A gracious presence summoned Isaiah into greater being as a person by calling him into a relationship that involved a mission. The question here was not "what will go for us?" but "who will go for us?"

When we become aware of the presence of God we also become aware of ourselves as a persons. This was the question Moses raised as he experienced the presence of God: "Who am I that I should go to Pharaoh?" (Exod. 3:1–15). And when God wanted to be identified to Moses, God did not do so by means of a string of theological abstractions, but by identification in personal relationship — God was the God of Abraham, Isaac, and Jacob. And throughout the pages of the four Gospels we see Jesus meeting persons in terms of who they were, in personal relationships that reached toward individual need. He was constantly calling upon people to measure their relationship with themselves, with others, and with God against the quality of God's personal relation to them. To God they were "who" or "thou," not things or an it.

It is my purpose to identify the pastoral approach with the "who" rather than with the "what." But let us first distinguish between them a little more clearly. When we ask, "What is the human person?" we are lumping all people together and asking about common traits. The answer is then to be found in generalizations in which the individual person is lost. "All people are sinners" is just such a generalization. It may be true enough, but the meaning of the actual personal experience of sin is lost. Such an approach makes the individual one of a class, and it thus reduces the person to a thing. It leads to concepts of a deterministic nature, whether answered in theological or psychological terms. It robs the individual of uniqueness and detracts from the personal quality of existence. A generalization of this kind has certain values, but it is completely inadequate as a basis for the communication of the gospel, for the gospel concerns a living relationship and is communicated in its deeper levels through relationship.

When we ask the "who" question we move from the general to the particular, from humankind to a human being, a person, a unique, experiencing being of dignity and worth. The "who" question can never be answered in the abstract, but only in a personal relation. "Who do you say that I am?" asked Christ, not what (Matt. 16:13–15). To answer this question his disciples had to enter into a personal relationship with him, through which they also discovered something of who they were. No person can tell you who you are, but each person you meet demands something of you which, in turn, to some extent creates who you are. Thus the relationship between a mother and a child brings to each of them a new self, a new being. Likewise the relationship between friends, between husband and wife, between pastor and person, between person and God. "If any one is in Christ he is a new creation" (2 Cor. 5:17). In such a relationship we experience ourselves as autonomous persons called upon to choose, and in our choices and decisions we become something we have not already been.

When we ponder the meaning of who we are as distinct from what we are, we may discover that concentrating on the "what" question is really an escape from responsibility. For we can describe ourselves and others in endless abstractions without coming anywhere near our own experience. Or we can talk endlessly on an intellectual level about the meaning of life without ever facing the personal meaning of our own existence. To see ourselves as one of a class removes the anxiety that accompanies the sense of personal uniqueness or individuality. The tendency to conformity in our culture has been commented upon frequently. It is one thing to describe oneself as a sinner like all others. It is quite another thing to become aware of the actual experience of sin in our own life, to come to ourselves as the Prodigal came to himself and face the decision that such awareness demands. All of us would like to be lost in the crowd, but salvation comes only in becoming what God in divine wisdom intended us to become as individual persons. We meet the God who is in Christ only in personal relationship, and in this meeting we become new persons. But we can become so engrossed in the intellec-

tual concepts and generalizations of the faith, in the answers
to the "what" questions, that we successfully avoid the deeper
responsibilities of "who?"

The Person as Spirit

In speaking of the "what" and "who" of persons, we are dealing with a biblical insight into human nature — our aspect as
creature on the one hand, and as spirit on the other. The biblical account of Creation links humankind solidly with biological creation. Adam's physical body was created first; then God
"breathed into his nostrils the breath of life; and man became a
living being" (Gen. 2:7). We share the physical and organismic
levels of life with other living creatures. As such we are subject
to the processes of birth and death, to suffering and pain, and to
many other contingencies of existence. But human beings are
distinctive because we know an existence on another level —
as a living soul, made, according to the Genesis account, "in
the image of God." Here the "soul" expresses the ultimate dimension in human nature, which would include not only our
capacity for self-awareness and self-transcendence but also our
capacity for awareness of the presence of God and of meaning
on a level beyond that of our earthly existence. With this there
is also a unique capacity for a level of autonomy. We have the
degree of freedom to accept or reject demands, relationships, or
meanings perceived as being the will of God.

But human beings are not a dualism; we are a unity. And
the unity or synthesis of body and soul has been called "spirit."
For what is "breathed into man," that is, what is given to us
in relationships, comes through the bodily as well as through
the "soulish" dimensions of our being. And how we receive,
assimilate, and give unique expression to grace in our relationships, is accomplished through the physical as well as through
the "soulish" dimensions of our being. From a Christian point
of view, to the usual levels of psychosomatic unity (chemical,
physical, mental, social, environmental) must be added "spirit,"
the human spirit, as the crowning level. The human spirit is the
synthesis of unity (or failure of unity) of our total being in relation to ourselves, to others, and to God expressed in terms of
meaning, value, and obligation. It is the spirit of a person of

which we are really speaking when we ask, Who is he? Who is she? Our personal identity is the synthesis, or dynamic organization, of our total being as it has emerged through our human and divine relationships. Our identity is also the expression of our spirit.

By spirit then we mean the self, or person, in the dynamic synthesis and meaning that we possess within ourselves and in our relationships with others.[2] Whatever transcendent qualities we understand as belonging to the self, or spirit, we must see as undeveloped potentials that achieve healthy growth or distortion in the crucible of human relationships beginning at birth. This is the corrective that empirical psychology applies to a religious concept of self that sees the self divorced from the total processes of becoming. The self is the expression of the organic unity of the individual, not a separate entity. What happens on the physical level of our life then affects our self, or spirit, just as what happens to us as whole persons will affect our physiological functioning. The problem as to how a part of the individual gains control of the whole person, as in illness, and how the self, or spirit, may regain control and reorganize the functions of the parts of an individual, is elucidated by our understanding of the processes of illness on the one hand, and the processes of therapy or cure on the other.

This brings us to a statement of the central need of a person, or self, a question that is at the core of our concept of pastoral care. We can state this very simply. It is the need for us to become ourselves, to fulfill the image of God within us, to give actuality to the potential for which we were created. But such fulfillment cannot be described in any final or static terms, since we are dealing with constantly moving and changing life processes. It must be formulated in terms of living relationships — the individual in relation to God, in relation to other persons, and in relation to ourselves. This means formulation in terms of being rather than of doing, in terms of Paul's "fruits of the Spirit" rather than in terms of acts or behavior.

The concept of the needs of persons in pastoral care must also take into account what is understood today as empirical needs, that is, those needs learned in experience. Psychologists have formulated a concept of learned needs. There has been some discussion of learned needs in contrast to basic or inborn needs. Psychologists, may ignore the ultimate dimension, and this is justifiable as long as we recognize that their point of view does not give a full account of human nature. Pastoral care should take into consideration the needs of persons that arise on the empirical level. However, an adequate theory of pastoral care cannot be based only on a formulation of learned needs, but must see human beings in their ultimate dimensions. An illustration of what we mean is the concept of the need for love. Some psychologist may formulate this need solely in terms of experience, without any reference to human nature. However, in the New Testament the need for love is firmly grounded in the nature of God and the human being, but it is also elaborated — experientially — in religious rather than in psychological terms. The psychologist may indicate that the need for love is learned through the love of the mother, but the New Testament adds another dimension, that is, we love because we are first loved by God.

The central need of persons has been thought of by theology as salvation. We are sinners standing in need of salvation. This concept has suffered a certain distortion — viewed from the perspective of persons — because sin has become defined as actions, not relationships, that is, statically, not dynamically. Salvation has also been made a fixed experience, contingent upon accepting a given verbal formulation of the Christian faith, or undergoing a certain type of emotionally conditioned experience, or adhering to certain ritualistic forms. All these approaches are characterized by legalism in one form or another. But many persons who have found "salvation" through these approaches have not found fulfillment. They found no inner peace, no freedom from moralism, no release of their capacity to love, and very frequently the sense of forgiveness they experienced was a matter of repression of guilt feelings rather than release from such feelings in a new and creative relationship. The idea of salvation as a fulfillment of the self before itself, before other persons, and before God — or the actualization of something of the image of God — produces a kind of existential anxiety to which many respond by seeking refuge in static formulations that at least have the virtue of seeming concrete. But if pastoral care is to be concerned with the genuine cure of souls, it must see its function as that of helping persons to become what in

God's creative wisdom God intended them to become. This is not merely following a blueprint for human life, but living out a personal existence in a genuine relationship of trust and love.

Theology and Pastoral Care

This concept of pastoral care throws light on a problem that has come to the fore in recent years: the insistent by both pastors and theologians that theological concepts must be utilized more fully in pastoral care. Certain persons in the pastoral care movement have been criticized for being too psychologically oriented and not enough theologically so. Some authors have advanced the idea that pastoral care is really theological conversation with an individual, whereas preaching is theological conversation with a group.[3] So far none of these books has really clarified the issues involved, except that pastoral care must become a form of theological indoctrination! But is it not yet clear that we may be thoroughly indoctrinated in a given theological or moralistic position and still lose our own soul, and that indoctrination in itself may contribute heavily to the loss of the self?

Part of the problem here is a confusion of method. Theology is a method of interpreting Christian experience in intellectual terms. It states this interpretation in terms that are assumed to be universally valid. Thus it seeks to answer the "what" question. There is a real value in this as long as we understand the method and purpose of theological interpretation. But we must remember that the process moves in one direction, from experience to interpretation, and not from interpretation to experience. In this process of transformation, energy flows to the symbol, not from the symbol. The Christian faith is the experience of a relationship, including all of the processes involved in such a relationship. The fact that many persons have given intellectual assent to an interpretation, to a creed or a doctrine, or to an institution, in the belief that they have found salvation, only proves our point. For these persons have found only a kind of verbal or legal salvation; they have not found the freedom of the gospel to become their real selves.

Intellectual assent to a doctrine without experiencing of the personal relationship implied in the doctrine is responsible for the split between theological beliefs and life processes that is often observed in persons. Intellectually, such persons believe that God loves them, but they do not experience this in personal relationships. Or they may accept the Christian faith creedally as it was preached to them, but their lives are controlled by fear. An example of this is to be found in the words of a pastor, a man who felt ineffective and anxious in spite of fine intellectual abilities and personal talents. About himself he says,

> There is no question about guilt feelings arising out of any sense of satisfaction I find in my work. This fight is in myself. It relates to my concept of the Christian life, of sin and salvation. I have no problem here philosophically nor theologically. I understand that the love of God does involve some self-regard. But my emotions do not fit in. I don't know why. The experience has not accompanied the concept. I have never experienced salvation as a life process. But philosophically I have not found any better system. But I have not gotten these together. I read Kierkegaard and find that he had the same problem. Underneath I am sure that this causes me real pain, but consciousness won't admit the pain to court.[4]

When this man says that the experience has not accompanied the concept, he is speaking for us all. For experience never accompanies the concept unless there is at the same time a personal relationship that gives the concept reality in the deeper levels of our being.

The method of the theologian is that of interpretation, but the method of the genuine pastor is that of personal relationships, using interpretation to give intellectual substance to a reality that has been or is being experienced. And when the theologians become pastors, as sometimes they do, they move from the level of concepts to the level of personal relations.

We have spoken of the necessity for pastors to be involved in the experiences of persons. This means that pastors should not only preach about such things as sin, suffering, love, and forgiveness, but they must meet, in the pulpit and out of it, individuals in a personal relationship that makes it possible for them to become aware of, and talk about, "my sin," "my suffering," "my need for love and forgiveness," or "my need to be forgiving." In other words, we must know and understand the language of personal experience — what people mean when they say, "I think," "I feel," "I am," "I hate," "I love," "I fear," "I ought." Also language is used to conceal personal experience and its meaning, and pastors must learn to listen to this also and understand what it means. And pastors must learn to feel with other people, and to sense how they themselves would respond if they were in a similar situation as well as how the others are responding. The pastor's own perceptions of life and its meaning may not correspond to those of another person, but pastors must learn to deal with others in terms of the way in which others are perceiving themselves and their situation.

A large part of the personal relations that constitute pastoral care is the experience of communicating. Individuals need to be able to communicate or reveal themselves to the pastor and find their revelation accepted and understood. Only then can the pastor's communication or conversation be guided by a genuine understanding of the gospel as it relates to this particular individual's existence. Genuine pastoral care demands that pastors cease subjecting individuals to the various mass-production methods that have been developed in our churches and begin to deal with persons in terms of their own individual experience in the light of the gospel. Pastors need to learn to understand the language by which persons, including ourselves, reveal themselves and also conceal themselves.

Dimensions of Persons

We turn now to certain dimensions of "personhood" that are important for pastoral care.

One dimension that the pastor must learn to respect is privacy. As a basic characteristic of persons, privacy is a function of individuality. To be an individual means to draw boundaries, or to seek boundaries where the self begins and ends. Psychoanalysts often speak of ego-boundaries. Here we are thinking of privacy as an essential dimension of persons in which the self learns to distinguish itself from what is not itself, and to form some relationship to each. One essential power of the self is the ability to exclude or to take in, to define its own being as distinct from, but in relation to, what is not self.

The dimension of privacy, under the stimulus of anxiety, often becomes elaborately defensive: a wall is built around the self and "no trespassing" signs erected to keep even ourselves out. The various defense mechanisms elaborated by psychoanalysis function to this end. Thus the basic dimension of privacy becomes distorted in ways that restrict or even destroy the growth of the self. Because we have been hurt, made to feel anxious, or deprived of satisfactions in our personal relationships, we respond defensively and want to keep others out. A sense of the disapproval of others, and even of a part of ourselves, causes us to keep some of our own feelings and wishes hidden even from ourselves. If someone tries to invade this area of privacy, we become anxious and build our defenses higher. Or if we open ourselves out of coercion, we then build up resentments against the intruder. Often our prayers are shallow because we cannot permit even God to enter the area of ourselves that we wish to conceal.

With this deep sense of privacy, we live in a community of persons. Our very personhood depends on our relationships with others. There is no way we can fulfill our destiny as persons by isolated self-manipulation, even though we would like to do so. Our destiny is to become part of others and permit others to become part of us. This is community, Christian community, to which the alternative is emotional and spiritual impoverishment. As persons, then, we have a deep need for privacy, for exercising the prerogative of individuality to set its own boundaries. But we also live in a community of persons. For growth, health, and fulfillment the dimension of privacy needs to function in the direction of openness to ourselves, to others, and to God. Openness is the opposite of defensiveness and is grounded in trust. Trust, according to Erikson, is learned in infancy, in the first stage of growth. It is only through openness that we can take in, assimilate, utilize, or discard what others have to give to us. To become a person is to live in tension between the need for privacy and the need to be open, a tension that is continually being overcome by trust. Growing persons learn to test the power of reality to inflict emotional injury, to take certain risks of being hurt, to stake out less and less of themselves as private, and to develop increasing openness and transparency before others. Effective pastors, through the quality of their relationships, enable others to lower their defenses and become increasingly open. This may be a problem for pastors, since their privacy is constantly being intruded upon, and they may respond negatively to others for this reason. Also, openness may be pushed to a pathological degree through the compulsion to exhibit our emotional and spiritual anatomy as a means of manipulating others.

The kind of love manifest in Christ was a self-giving love, not a demanding, manipulative, possessive, or controlling love. This is the kind of love that makes it possible for others to be open to us, that is, as open as the specific forces of their being permit them to be at any given moment. Not all persons could open themselves to Christ, and some will not be able to open themselves to any pastor, nor permit the pastor to be open to them. But the meaning of Christian love is that a relationship is offered that accepts the other as a person. One thing such acceptance means is that privacy is respected. Acceptance on such terms helps to make it possible for persons to respond with some degree of openness. Until they themselves are ready, we cannot advance further without doing harm. At such times we need to learn to relax and trust in the work of the Holy Spirit, for the Holy Spirit functions at the point where persons are struggling to overcome their privacy and accept fellowship in a community. "Behold, I stand at the door and knock. If any one hears my voice and opens the door, I will come in to him and eat with him and he with me." This deep insight expresses respect for the privacy of persons, but it also emphasizes our need for fellowship, and it indicates that fellowship is available. Pastors mediate the redemptive love of God in a measure when they respect the privacy of a person while at the same time offering something of themselves in an understanding, accepting relationship. Only genuine openness on the part of pastors will allay anxieties in others and enable them to become open to relationship.

Another dimension in which persons experience themselves is uniqueness. By uniqueness we do not mean a sense of superiority or grandiosity. Neither do we mean the kind of fantasy that some persons have of themselves — the man who prayed and thanked God that he was not like others (Luke 18:9–14). These are pathological expressions.

Our uniqueness means that we are called to become ourselves before God, that we have the gift of life with all of its possibilities from God and the responsibility of developing this potential. Psychologists speak of individuation, which involves the achievement of uniqueness. Christian theology speaks about our being created in the image of God, and the Gospels about investing and multiplying one's talents. However we describe it, each person has a uniqueness that we are called upon to fulfill.

But we have this uniqueness along with much in common with other persons. In many ways we are very much alike. We live in a culture that pressures us into conformity, which in turn leads us to deny our individuality. Because of our common characteristics there can be a science and a theology of the human person. But our uniqueness cannot be formulated or generalized. It is not to be found in any book. It is to be found only in a living experience in which our relationship with ourselves, with others, and with God constantly calls us to change and growth. And this involves at times considerable renunciation and pain.

The need for becoming oneself, for fulfilling our uniqueness in some degree, has been recognized by many. For example, uniqueness is stressed by Carl Rogers in his book *On Becoming a Person*.[5] It is also emphasized by existentialists like Rollo May,[6] and, in terms of the concept of self-actualization, it is central in the formulations of Maslow.[7] But fulfilling one's uniqueness, or finding self-actualization, is not something to be achieved in isolation, but only in relationship with others. We become ourselves only in and through others and they become themselves only in and through us. The mother finds a part of her uniqueness through her child, and the child through the mother. This is emphasized by Paul Tillich when he speaks of becoming oneself both as an individual and as a member of the group.[8] Individuality and community are the two poles of self-realization, and these are always in dynamic tension. Psychoanalysis is an elaborate system for interpreting the intricacies of this process. In Christian theology the individual is seen in relation to the fellowship of the church, the Christian community, and the Kingdom of God. The Christian faith, with its emphasis on the relationships of individuals before God, is equipped to recognize and foster uniqueness.

The redemptive, self-giving love that is in Christ respects the need for all persons to become themselves, that is, to develop their uniqueness, or to fulfill their potential. Redemptive love does not pressure persons into conformity of action or belief. It recognizes that we do not have the answers for the questions and problems of others; we may, however, have the power to relate to others in a way that helps them to find their own answers, to find the truth that is themselves before God. This is living truth, a truth manifested in relationships. This is life in the Spirit, not in the law. Amid all the pressures of conformity in our culture, Christian pastors should offer a relationship that opens the possibility for persons to become themselves before God. It is tragic when a church and its pastors so reinforce the static expectancies of our culture, that young persons, struggling with the problem of becoming themselves, can say, "All my life I have had to be what others — my parents, teachers, pastor, and others — said I should be, so that now I do not know who I am or who I want to be. I only know I do not want to be what others tell me I should be." Christian experience calls us, not to conformity to this world, but to a kind of transformation that comes from the constant renewing of the mind and spirit in growing commitment to the Spirit of God. Again, only pastors who are genuinely advancing toward becoming their real selves before others and before God will be able to communicate to others, particularly to children and youth, the strength that will enable them to become themselves before God. Such pastors will also arouse considerable hostility in those who are rigidly anxious and who alleviate their anxiety by conforming. But as we learn to deal with hostility in love and understanding, we will become part of the redemptive process in some of these persons also.

A third dimension of persons is awareness. Awareness involves a sensitivity to our own inner world and to the external world, including other persons. Through awareness we bring into consciousness the meaning of our relationships and experiences; we know them in a direct, living sense, and hence we are able to cope with negative meaning and to enhance positive meaning. Awareness is a direct knowledge of the living truth at work within us, as distinguished from knowledge about ourselves. Awareness involves insight, and insight is grounded in strength and trust. It is through awareness that we fulfill our capacity for self-acceptance, self-understanding, and self-transcendence.

Awareness is developed very gradually from birth. At some time during the first year of life we become aware of others as distinct from ourselves. Mothers see the first signs of such awareness. Awareness of the self, of others, and of the meaning of experiences in relation to others is stimulated by satisfaction of needs at the hands of others, and also by frustration, conflict, and suffering. Such negative experiences may bring so much pain that the child turns away in denial and fantasy. The growing self is crippled to the extent that this happens. But awareness is an essential aspect of the self, and the self grows in part through becoming aware. The pastor constantly meets persons who are struggling to become aware of themselves, their motivations, the meaning of their relationships, and especially the meaning of their suffering, but who also find strong tendencies in themselves to avoid awareness.

A person, then, does not have to become aware. Freud shocked the world when he introduced his concept of repression. What is repression? It is a reaction of the self in which memories, feelings, and meanings are blotted out of consciousness; it is a blocking of the process of awareness. Awareness admits the raw material of life into consciousness, while repression pushes it back. Repression operates when the self is too weak to deal with issues or when aspects of experience are too painful. But memories, feelings, and meanings of which we are unconscious may seriously influence our existence. Indeed, this is part of the meaning of neurotic illness — the reactions of persons are being determined by memories and feelings of which they are not aware and hence do not understand and cannot control. Neurotic symptoms are expressions of repressed, unconscious material that has gained control in some disguised, symbolic form. Thus awareness is necessary to the control and direction of ourselves as persons. It also plays a significant part in our religious experience. Before we pray to be forgiven for our sins, for example, we should pray for strength to become aware of what our real sins are. We cannot confess sins of which we are not aware!

The depth of awareness of our relationships and their meaning forms the basis of our responses. For awareness, or insight, is our response; it is the way in which we take in meaning, assimilate it, and act upon it. This is at least part of what Tillich seems to mean when he talks about taking anxiety into oneself.[9] The obstacle to taking anxiety into the self is the pain involved. But the self gains in strength as the self is able to become aware of its negative feelings and deal constructively with them. This means courageously facing the threatening forces within one's being and within one's relationships with others.

The psychologist is likely to speak of perception rather than of awareness. The difference is that perception is an operational psychological concept, while awareness is in the experience of a person. The problem of perception and its relation to personality factors has received and is receiving much attention in psychology. To what extent do personality factors such as feelings or desire color our perception of our inner and our external worlds? Distortions of perception are especially likely to occur where strong feeling such as fear, hate, or love is involved. The problem of perception is important to communication since it focuses attention on the way in which communication is received, and on why communications are often misunderstood. Perception is another way of formulating the problem of awareness.

From the experimental and clinical study of perception comes some confirmation of ideas held by several representatives of the dynamic point of view. Witkin and his associates, in *Personality through Perception,* report the results of some experimental research in perception. They define the function of perception as that of separating an item from its field or context. Individual differences in the ability to separate an item from its context are related to the aggressive or passive character of the personality structure. Individuals who are dependent in their interpersonal relations are "field dependent" in their perceptual functioning, while those who are more aggressive and independent perceive objects more independently of the field. The authors describe these persons as follows:

Field-dependent persons tend to be characterized by passivity in dealing with the environment; by unfamiliarity with and fear of their own impulses, together with poor control over them; by lack of self-esteem; and by the possession of a relatively primitive, undifferentiated body image. Independent or analytically perceptual performers, in contrast, tend to be characterized by activity and independence in relation to the environment; by closer communication with, and better control of, their own impulses; and by relatively high self-esteem and a more mature, differentiated body image.[10]

These findings tend to confirm the general thesis that personality functions as a whole, and that the patterns of response that operate on one level tend to operate on all levels. Our perception of objects and our perception of persons and values do not follow essentially different patterns. Perception and response are governed by the same needs, defenses, and self-image. Indeed, perception is part of the response, since it is our own creation of our world, partly in terms of our own needs. There is a sense in which we create our world after our own image, a replica of our own unconscious. Or in other words, our perceived world becomes a symbol through which our own unconscious meanings, values, and prejudices, anxieties, guilts, and confusions, find expression.

Pastors will deal with many persons who are searching for awareness of meaning in their lives. Some will be very dependent and want quick and easy answers, and we will be tempted to give such answers. But we will soon find that such answers are of little avail, for while they may be understood and accepted intellectually, they are powerless to penetrate to the deeper levels of being. Other persons will be in conflict, they will both want and not want to achieve insight. They will want insight insofar as they want relief from their suffering, but they will not want it insofar as insight involves their facing their suffering and coming to some kind of terms with that suffering. Particularly difficult for them will be the kind of insight that reveals their attitudes toward themselves and others that they feel the need to justify or defend. Only through patience and understanding will pastors be able to help such people, since they will perceive pastors also in terms of their own needs and patterns. It is for this reason that at times a long, self-giving relationship is necessary in order to help persons correct their own misperceptions of the pastor, or of others, from within. One of the goals of psychotherapy is the increase of awareness.

The problem of perception or awareness has real importance for the communication of the gospel. Involved in such communication is not only the awareness of the pastor, how pastors perceive themselves and the gospel and those to whom they speak, but also the factors that control the awareness of the hearers. Often the message proclaimed verbally is received and perceived by the hearers in a quite different manner than was intended. We hear and see what we are emotionally ready to hear and see.

Jesus faced and struggled with the problem of the level of awareness and of handicaps to clear perception in those with whom he dealt. He sought to help people to gain insight into their attitudes toward themselves, toward others, and toward God; but he found it very difficult. When he spoke in parables his disciples asked him for an explanation of the meaning, a common defense against insight. He spoke of their having their hearts hardened; that is, they could not be aware of what they were feeling nor of the factors controlling their perceptions. Seeing, they did not see; and hearing, they did not hear; nor did they understand. It is only through seeing, hearing, and understanding on the deeper levels of our being that we are healed.

Certainly one of the goals of pastoral care is to help persons gain a deeper awareness of themselves and of their relationship to others and to God, both actual and potential. This involves insight into their inner conflicts, and how they tend to use others in a manipulative, controlling manner. It also involves an awareness of the dimension of sin and its problems — not in the abstract, but in its concrete manifestation in their experience. But it would need to go beyond this and help persons to awareness of the meaning of salvation in terms of love toward God and others. In accomplishing this, the depth of awareness or insight of the pastor will be a determining factor; the pastor's own lack of insight will get in the way. But when pastors become concerned with what they are communicating through their relationships, and measure their words in this light, they will begin to help persons find strength. A Christian church ought to be a place where persons are expanding their awareness of meaning, not a place where repression is encouraged. It is through awareness that the Holy Spirit functions to lead us into truth.

A fourth dimension of persons that is significant for pastoral care is autonomy.

By autonomy we do not mean "absolute" freedom. As we study human life we cannot help but become aware of the numerous levels of the determinants — biological, psychological, social, philosophical — that to a measure control our behavior either in a positive or a negative fashion.[11] But even from the biological sciences comes evidence that a living organism possesses spontaneity, that is, the ability to control its responses from within itself, to act on its environment as well as to react to its environment.

Interpreters of human behavior from an existential point of view understand the potential for autonomy as an inherent element in human existence.[12] Psychotherapeutic psychology seems to be very deterministic in its formulations, but it assumes sufficient autonomy on the part of patients to permit them the decision to move into therapy and to make certain necessary decisions about themselves along the way. Christian theology has held to a large element of freedom, but it has not been blind to deterministic elements in human beings.[13]

The tendency to put autonomy and determinism in opposition, where accepting one concept means rejecting the other, is mistaken. Personal existence is lived in a tension between these opposites. Perhaps it would be more accurate to say that we are determined by many inner and external forces, but that we also have the potential for autonomy. Paul insisted on freedom in Christ, but it was he who wrote, "Whatever a man sows, that he will also reap" (Gal. 6:7). Here he is speaking deterministically. Today we could reinterpret that sentence and add, whatever is sown in a child, that will be reaped in later life. The potential for autonomy is developed through experience, and many children are denied the kind of human relationships that make this possible. They become adults with the inability to act autonomously, or at least with a low degree of functioning autonomy. To the extent that we have failed to develop autonomy or have lost it, we are sick. The pastor needs to sense the limits of people's ability to exercise their autonomy, and not expect of them, at a given moment, a level of autonomous behavior of which they are not capable. It is also the function of the Christian faith to help persons expand the functioning limits of their autonomy.

Since autonomy is a function of the human ego, the next question is that of the nature of the ego, considered both psychologically and theologically.

Theologically it is often assumed that the ego, or self, is bad. This is often interpreted to be the meaning of Jesus' statements about self-denial (Matt. 16:25). In these interpretations the self is often considered as evil, a thing to be denied. Such interpretations fail to make a very necessary distinction, probably because they grow out of a basic antagonism toward pleasurable human impulses. These objections are really aimed at an aspect of persons that is expressed in Freud's term "narcissism," which means an infantile feeling of self-love, worth, and power, and the need to organize the entire universe around oneself. Freud pointed out that the process of growth consists in part in giving up a large measure of narcissism and learning to relate to objects, particularly to other persons, in terms of themselves.[14] In this sense certain infantile aspects of the self do need to be denied or renounced, in order that a person may grow to more mature levels. The potential for this growth is inherent in the real ego or self, but requires certain qualities of human relationship for fulfillment. To help persons understand the necessity for giving up immature satisfactions for the sake of more mature experiences is sound. Or to help them see that commitment to Christ involves denying or modifying those aspects of the self that are in conflict with the spirit of Christ is also sound. But to preach that they must deny the real self and become "selfless" is to teach persons that they must be less than human — puppets either on the strings of their own unconscious impulses or of some environmental power.

But the real issue between Christian theological and modern psychological concepts of the ego or self is on a different point. For Christian theology holds to a nonempirical self, a self transcendent to experience while partaking in experience, a given out of which growth occurs.[15]

On the other hand, psychological theories of the self have been empirical, their content depending on specific points of view.[16] In Freud's thought, for example, the ego becomes differentiated as infants find themselves in conflict between their impulses and external reality, and the function of the ego is to test reality and to discover some kind of solution of the conflict. In the infant the ego is considered very weak, and its growth depends upon wholesome relationships and the resolution of conflict. With the development of the superego, the ego faces the new task of reconciling impulses and wishes with demands and prohibitions. Here is some of the origin of intrapsychic conflict, the other part being the possibility of conflict between elements of the ego itself.

There would seem to be no question as to the empirical nature of ego development. This means that the way in which we function in perceiving inner or external reality, our ability to test this reality and to relate to it in terms of its demands and also ours own needs, our ability to project solutions of our conflict in our imagination, our ability to make decisions and carry them out in action — these and other such capacities are the product of learning. Indeed, Sullivan would define the self in terms of "security operations"; that is, the self develops out of the need for the person to master anxiety.[17]

It should be noted here that the experience of conflict and evil is central in both the Christian and the Freudian account of the self. The biblical account of Creation in Genesis sees human awareness emerging out of conflict between aspects within ourselves (Adam debated whether or not he should eat the apple) and between ourselves and the Creator. The empirical point of view disregards ultimate relationships but understands the ego to emerge through conflict with other persons, beginning with the mother, and it sees the conflicts here in terms both of those that are inevitable because of the human situation and of those produced because of immaturities within the mother. In other words, on either level the problem of the ego is the problem of relationships, both what it receives and how it responds, and how it deals with conflict. The ego is the totality of those processes that seek to synthesize inner needs and conflicts with outer demands, frustrations, and value. The self is the ego subjectively experienced.

But there is a growing tendency today in psychological circles to consider a nonempirical aspect of the self. Karen Horney describes "the real self as that central inner force, common to all human beings yet unique in each, which is the deep source of growth."[18]

Several psychoanalysts, of which Heinz Hartmann is a leader, have expanded Freud's theory of the ego to make room for a "conflict-free" aspect of the ego that functions according to its own spontaneous nature.[19] In other words, here is a concept of ego functions that exist prior to conflict and are not dependent upon conflict for their functioning.

Hartmann begins with a period prior to the experience of conflict, when the ego and the id are still undifferentiated. The ego thus partakes of the hereditary factors that are recognized as the root of instinctive drives. Hartmann believes that the ego and its functions (perception, motility, memory, thinking) are grounded on laws of maturation that are part of their nature and not derived from the instincts. While relationships and conflicts with the external world are seen to play a large part in the actual growth of the ego, yet there is still a "conflict-free" portion that functions according to its own laws. These "autonomous factors" are termed "primary ego autonomy." But the ego may find itself in conflict, and to resolve the conflict may utilize the defense mechanism of reaction formation and, for example, adopt the attitude of altruism to cover up deep feelings of resentment. Later, the conflict may be resolved, but the attitude of altruism remains. This Hartmann calls "secondary autonomy," and he considers it a highly important process in the development of the stability of personality. The same "secondary autonomy" may occur in relation to other defense mechanisms. Or the opposite may occur, and the ego may hold onto destructive behavior after the original conflict that produced the behavior has been resolved. The problem here is that of the reversibility and irreversibility of structure. It is important to note that Hartmann considers the synthetic or integrating function of the ego to belong to that area which is governed by primary autonomy.

Autonomy of the ego is not be confused with conscious self-direction or rational choice, although these may be involved. On the other hand, much that passes for rational decision may be really pseudo-autonomy. For example, persons acting under a strong compulsion may insist that they are acting out of autonomy. Autonomous integrating functions operate on a level deeper than rational processes, and we are conscious, not that we are integrating ourselves, but that integration is taking place within us. We experience this as something being done to us rather than as something we are doing. And yet we also recognize this change as something that is the result of processes within ourselves, and which for us is a valid and authentic experience. We do not see it as due to outside control, just as we do not see it as the result of a conscious decision.

In such experiences we may be aware of a new mastery of our impulses, or perhaps of a modification of some overscrupulous part of our conscience. A kind of impulsive behavior, for example, that has been a problem no longer occurs. Or we may be aware of a new strength and a fresh approach to a reality problem; a new way of relating, for example, to authority figures that had previously given us problems. This new strength and its resulting change of behavior are experienced not as the result of our own conscious effort but as being received. There is also a new sense of responsibility, meaning the ability to respond in depth in a constructive rather than in a destructive manner in personal relationships.

The relation of these interpretations to certain of those in Christian experience should not be missed. For there is much in Christian literature, and in the writings of the mystics, that sounds strangely like the experience of ego autonomy, even though it is expressed in other terms.[20] The Christian understanding has been that any changes taking place within a person are not the result of our conscious will (we cannot save ourselves), but rather the result of God working within us. Sometimes these changes are attributed to the work of the Holy Spirit, or God in us. Yet the testimony has been that we are most free or autonomous when we are most obedient to God. Only in a legalistic, compulsive type of religion is God understood as a being who reduces human freedom.

Genuine love toward God and toward self and others, when it is experienced, releases autonomous powers within the individual, and a new sense of strength and changed relationships are the result.

The communication of the gospel, or pastoral care, always needs to be given within the context of the autonomy of both the communicator and the recipient. The level of freedom or autonomy possessed by pastors will guide the amount of autonomy they will be able to allow others. If pastors are compulsively determined in their attitudes and relationships they will seek to bring others under their authority. The meaning of love, as pastors reveal it in their relationships, will be in part expressed in the quality of autonomy pastors are able to grant to others. Pastors may find themselves in real conflict between authoritative and autonomous principles.

On the other hand, pastors will deal with persons who are not, at a given moment, inwardly free to accept the love of God, or any relationship that involves autonomy. Such persons will understand God in authoritative, demanding terms, and will need a relationship on the human level to make the possibility of autonomous experience real to them. In their inability to be autonomous they will find themselves unable to make a fully Christian decision. Christian decisions that are made through pressures from others represent a pseudo autonomy and will lead to a neurotic condition if adhered to.

Part of the meaning of the grace of God is that we have the freedom to accept or reject what is given. Grace is never forced. For grace, which is God's free gift, given out of God's abundance and our need, respects us as autonomous persons. Too many persons in our churches have made their decisions about the Christian faith out of fear or guilt and have not experienced a positive motivation in their religious life. Pastoral care is genuinely effective when it permits persons to come to themselves and to make the decision that concerns their eternal destiny from within themselves.

The pastor is called upon to minister to persons caught in a culture that has developed strong pressures toward conformity, and at times to minister to persons caught in various forms of rebellion. Sometimes the church itself is organized to enforce conformity; it has the powerful sanctions of guilt and punishment, and sometimes of salvation in return for conformity. Sometimes the church is expected to reinforce patterns of conformity set by groups in the larger culture.

Pastors may see themselves as official enforcers of conformity and defenders of fixed standards, "the conscience of the community." Or they may feel the pressures of their congregation, or of their denominational body, or of their local community forcing them into conformity. One of the strong professional hazards

of young clergy today is the temptation to deny their individuality by conforming to standards set by powerful groups. To
the extent that pastors become victims of this pressure — and
most of us do at some point — pastors become powerless to
help others caught in the same web. While rebellion may save
persons from the evils of conformity, it has its own dangers and
inadequacies. The Christian faith calls for the development of
human potential in positive ways, through love and service and
sacrifice and courage. Only as pastors have found this path can
they lead others over it. And they need to see the task here on
both the individual and the group level. In a unique way the
pastor stands between individual and culture and is called upon
to mediate health and wholeness to each.

The Christian understanding of the meaning of grace takes
us into the very heart of human nature. For part of the idea
of grace involves the close dependence of human beings on our
Creator for life and sustenance, and on our Redeemer for an
understanding and experience of the kind of relationships that
bring fulfillment of ourselves as creatures. When we forget we
are creatures, dependent on the grace of God, we forge for ourselves an identity in which we seek to become God. But on the
other hand, when we experience the meaning of dependence on
God as persons and not as a things, and understand that part
of the gift of grace is the gift of autonomy or freedom, and that
accepting the grace of God means fulfilling our autonomy, then
the idea of dependence on God takes on a creative meaning. It
is not dependence as usually practiced in human relationships,
where the dependent individual neurotically surrenders autonomy. It is a relationship in which we recognize God as the source
of our being and all that fulfills that being, including the power
of decision. The doctrine of grace thus symbolizes our tremendous dependence on God, and in the light of our autonomy it
also symbolizes the interdependence of persons, rather than dependence on others. Experiences akin to grace may occur on
the human level when we receive from others love that may be
accepted without surrendering autonomy. But there is always
the ambiguous element in human relations that is not present
in the grace of God.

We have been speaking of a situation that is paradoxical.
When we experience autonomy in depth, it is as though what

is happening to us is a gift rather than the result of our own effort. Yet this is experienced as autonomy, or freedom. It is this experience that D. M. Baillie calls the "paradox of grace."[21]

Baillie points out that whenever through faith we understand God as the ultimate source of anything in our experience, "He comes in, as it were, on the vertical line from the eternal world to touch the horizontal line on which we inevitably have another explanation in empirical terms."[22] The Incarnation is the central paradox, he holds, since in it we see the life of God, but also a completely human life. Baillie's statement of the paradoxical nature of the Christian faith is important for our interpretation of pastoral care, since we are saying that it is the task of the pastor to communicate the gospel to persons at the point of both their ultimate and proximate needs. If the Christian faith has any meaning, it must be found in relation to the needs of personal existence. Any attempt to understand the relation between the Christian faith and modern psychotherapy must take this paradoxical situation into account; and it must recognize that beyond all formulations there is a mystery in faith that is beyond knowledge and that therefore resists all attempts at formulation. Of the paradox of grace, Baillie writes,

> Its essence lies in the conviction which a Christian man possesses, that every good thing in him, every good thing he does, is somehow not wrought by himself but by God. This is a highly paradoxical conviction, for in ascribing all to God it does not abrogate human personality nor disclaim personal responsibility. Never is human action more truly and fully personal, never does the agent feel more perfectly free, than in those moments of which he can say as a Christian that whatever good was in them was not his but God's.[23]

Paul's statement is taken as a classical expression of this paradox: "By the grace of God I am what I am, and his grace toward me was not in vain. On the contrary, I worked harder than any of them, though it was not I, but the grace of God which is with me" (1 Cor. 15:10).

The paradox of grace is an expression of the faith of Christians that the good that we achieve is somehow not through our own efforts, but through a creative energy or power that was given to us. As Christians we feel ourselves free and responsible, and accept failure as our own doing, but we see whatever good we accomplish as the working of God's power within us. Furthermore, we are not anxious at the demands of God, for we understand that God asks nothing that God does not also give the grace to fulfill.

The experience in which the paradox of grace becomes real cannot be produced in us by verbal descriptions of it. Grace is experienced in an I-Thou relationship with God in which we respond to God's self-giving love in wonder and gratitude and are able to accept ourselves in the light of God's acceptance of us. This does not mean that we become perfect persons, but living under the experience of grace should enable us to face, accept, and deal realistically with weaknesses. Grace never excuses us from responsibility; indeed, it places responsibility on us. Nor should we use our freedom to perpetuate destructive trends. Grace may bring to our awareness certain problems that we can work out only with the help of others, but this help will be accepted also as an expression of the grace of God. Thus it is not a weakness for a Christian to seek psychological or pastoral help. And the pastor who would give this help must be able to communicate grace and at the same time know how to deal with the empirical aspects of experience.

Earlier we indicated some possible objections to our interpretation of the work of the pastor as mediating the grace of God. One objection is that this concept is presumptuous; no human being can mediate God's grace. Behind this objection there is the tendency to discount or degrade the meaning of human relationships. This tendency can be very real and highly important to some persons because of harmful experiences with others who professed to love them. But the mediation of the grace of God does not require perfection in the pastor. Furthermore, it can never be done except from within the paradox of grace: I, yet not I, but the grace of God. As soon as we see ourselves as mediating God's love under our own power, we fail in communication. When we see that which we are able to be in relation to another as genuinely ourselves, yet not of ourselves, then some measure of the ultimate meaning of persons will be communicated with the immediate meaning.

Today there is emphasis on the "role of the minister," and some studies have indicated considerable confusion as to what the role of the minister really is. But there is a much deeper problem, and that is the profound fear in many ministers of the kind of spontaneous relationships with persons in which needs are felt and responses must be given. Because of this fear, ministers are inclined to "define their role" in the hope that clear definition will give a basis for action without the necessity of exposing themselves. But role-playing of this kind does not lead to genuine communication of the gospel. In its exaggerated forms such role-playing becomes playing God. The emptiness and futility of this is apparent. When pastors are able to forget their "role" as pastors and learn to give themselves — however little or much they have — genuinely, honestly, and spontaneously, as God gave in Christ, then the gospel will become a living issue to their people. Fear of honest spontaneity in human relationships is basically fear of the Holy Spirit and of its power in human life. It is the letter, the role, that kills; but the Spirit gives life.

We began this chapter with the questions, What is the human being? and Who is a person? The secret of communicating the gospel to persons at the point of their need is to meet them as persons in a relationship in which the paradoxical conditions of grace and personal responsibility find expression. We have not exhausted the dimensions of personal existence, but we have spoken of privacy, uniqueness, awareness, and autonomy as important in the process of being and becoming. The gospel must be communicated within these dimensions. This challenges pastors to learn the meaning of these dimensions in their own experience as persons. They will then have a basis for knowing what they mean to others.

What is the human being? We go to psychology and to Christian theology for answers to this question. Who is a person? Here we cannot depend on generalizations; we must go to persons themselves, in an understanding, mutually revealing relationship. We are the only creatures aware that we live in two worlds at the same time — the empirical and the ultimate. This dual orientation characterizes the unique potential of a person. It is not enough to communicate verbally the Christian answers to the questions arising in such an existence. The person must be met as a person, a Who, whether individually or in a group, and in the kind of relationship that mediates something of the nature and meaning of God to that person's empirical condition, whatever that happens to be. This is the meaning of pastoral care, the act of caring for persons in the spirit of Christ.

NOTES

1. The following is just part of a growing literature on the meaning of the personal relationship: Martin Buber, *I and Thou* (Edinburgh: T. & T. Clark, 1937); John Macmurray, *Persons in Relation* (New York: Harper & Row, 1961); Paul Tournier, *The Meaning of Persons* (New York: Harper & Row, 1957); Rollo May, with Ernest Angel and Henri F. Ellenberger, *Existence* (New York: Basic Books, Inc., 1958); William U. Snyder, *The Psychotherapy Relationship* (New York: Macmillan Company, 1961).

2. See Arnold B. Come, *Human Spirit and Holy Spirit* (Philadelphia: Westminster Press, 1959).

3. See Eduard Thurneysen, *A Theology of Pastoral Care* (Richmond, Va.: John Knox Press, 1962); Frederic Greeves, *Theology and the Cure of Souls* (Manhasset, N.Y.: Channel Press, 1962).

4. Personal communication.

5. Carl Rogers, *On Becoming a Person* (Boston: Houghton Mifflin Co., 1961).

6. Rollo May, *Existence*.

7. A. H. Maslow, *Motivation and Personality* (New York: Harper & Row, 1954).

8. Paul Tillich, *The Courage to Be* (New Haven: Yale University Press, 1952), chaps. 4 and 5.

9. Ibid., chap. 6.

10. H. A. Witkin, H. B. Lewis, M. Hertzman, K. Machover, P. Bretnall Meissner, and S. Wapner, *Personality through Perception* (New York: Harper & Row, 1954), p. 469.

11. Clyde Kluckhohn and Henry A. Murray, *Personality in Nature, Society and Culture* (New York: Alfred A. Knopf, 1953); Gordon Allport, *Pattern and Growth in Personality* (New York: Holt, Rinehart and Winston, 1961).

12. Rollo May, *Existence*.

13. Albert Outler, *Psychotherapy and the Christian Message* (New York: Harper & Row, 1954), chap. 2.

14. Sigmund Freud, *Collected Papers,* vol. 4 (London: Hogarth Press and the Institute for Psychoanalysis, 1956).

15. Albert Outler, *Psychotherapy and the Christian Message,* chap. 4.

16. Calvin S. Hall and Gardner Lindzey, *Theories of Personality* (New York: John Wiley and Sons, Inc., 1957).

17. Harry Stack Sullivan, *The Interpersonal Theory of Psychiatry* (New York: W. W. Norton and Co., 1953).

18. Karen Horney, *Neurosis and Human Growth* (New York: W. W. Norton and Co., 1950), p. 17.

19. Heinz Hartmann, *Essays on Ego Psychology* (New York: International Universities Press, 1964).

20. See "The Ego and Mystic Selflessness," by Herbert Fingarette, in *Identity and Anxiety,* ed. Maurice R. Stein, Arthur J. Vidich, and David Manning White (Glencoe, Ill.: Free Press, 1960).

21. D. M. Baillie, *God Was in Christ* (New York: Scribner's, 1955).

22. Ibid., p. 110.

23. Ibid., p. 114.

≺ 4 ≻

Further Considerations

THE CONCEPT OF PASTORAL CARE as developed by Eduard Thurneysen in *A Theology of Pastoral Care* is in direct contrast to the one we are developing. To Thurneysen, pastoral care means conversation. Its content is the same as the content of preaching, "a specific communication to the individual of the message proclaimed in general (i.e., to all) in the sermon to the congregation."[1] It is based on preaching and leads back to it. It is the communication of the "Word of God," a concept that appears constantly, and often with a vagueness of meaning, in Thurneysen's book. Essentially it seems to mean the content of his particular theology, for it soon becomes evident that the pastoral care of Roman Catholicism and of Pietism is totally unacceptable because it is grounded in different theologies. Pastoral counseling is "listening to the Word of God and responding to the Word of God."[2] Psychology is important for listening to a person, but immediately the pastor must challenge human meaning by questions directed from the Word of God. Listening is not for the sake of understanding the person but rather for the sake of gaining a vantage point from which to make a theological critique. This is described as the "breach" in the pastoral conversation — the analysis of human meaning in the light of the Word of God, that is, according to the theological beliefs of the pastor.

Thurneysen has trouble with the human side of pastoral care. He agrees that persons must accept and respond to the gospel, yet under the transcendent sovereignty of God human beings can do nothing for themselves. The pastor cannot speak the Word through his or her own efforts or thought: "He does not speak out of his own depths, but he speaks with all the power given him by that alien Word now conferred upon him; he speaks the Word of God."[3]

The pastoral relationship is not an important consideration for Thurneysen. Pastoral conversation is the central element in his approach. The relationship is left largely to implication. Pastors are interested, sympathetic, and concerned for the person. They see themselves as standing under the same judgment as the person, an idea that is shared by other points of view. However, the relationship is an adjunct of the pastoral conversation rather than, as we are interpreting it, the basis for the conversation.

Not until the final chapter does Thurneysen discuss the relationship as such. This relationship becomes one of mutual trust through the word of forgiveness under which both pastor and person stand in relation to God. The great danger, he holds, is that of mutual dependence. Pastoral care must avoid any human dependence since this may stand in the way of the one valid dependence, dependence on God. There Thurneysen identifies dependence with transference in the psychological sense. He admits that such dependences may be unavoidable and indicates that when such dependencies occur they must be recognized and dissolved. But he does not indicate how they are to be used for the benefit of the person. He makes no distinction between real and neurotic dependence, and nowhere in his discussion does he mention autonomy. He seeks to bind the person to God rather than to aid the person in outgrowing neurotic dependence and becoming autonomous. There is little room for human autonomy in his theological position.

There is no question but that the point of emphasis in Thurneysen's formulation is on the spoken word of the pastor, not on the person to whom the pastor is speaking. The person is very secondary in importance; the person is manipulated, theologically indoctrinated, and made dependent on the authority of the pastor. There is a kind of theological overintellectualization here that makes deep insight unnecessary. And one cannot escape the feeling that there is great dependence on the magic of words. Listening takes place in the light of the pastor's theology, not in terms of the meaning of existence to the person who is speaking. The stress of pastoral care is on guilt and forgiveness. We would accept this as very important, but not as the whole concern of the gospel with the needs of persons.

Thurneysen's interpretation of pastoral care is the logical outgrowth of his theological position. A rigid emphasis on the transcendent sovereignty of God and the nothingness of human beings, on the alien nature of God in relation to human beings, and on the power of verbal symbols seems to characterize his position. Such a position, if one can subscribe to it, does remove certain anxieties about the human situation and lift the despair created by fully accepted human responsibility. It also reduces human beings to puppets in the hands of the pastor and thus destroys their autonomy. Individuals are placed in the terrible position of rejecting God if they reject the words of the pastor. But they are also given reassurance that acceptance of verbal formulations will guarantee them eternal salvation.

Pastoral care, as we are developing it here, involves conversation, but more than conversation. Conversation, or dialogue,[4] is grounded in a relationship that makes such communication possible. In many pastoral conversations there is no real communication, or the communication may be negative. Communication in depth takes place when we enter into the experience of another person in terms of its meaning to us and, within this relationship, we say what is helpful or remain silent as the situation requires. Furthermore, it is not some kind of an "alien Word" that persons need for growth or redemption. It is the sense of the presence of a God who in Christ has become involved in the joys, the struggles, the suffering, and the destiny of human beings by becoming incarnate and fully participating in human existence. While the faith of the pastor must be strong and redemptive, theological formulations must be subject to examination in the light of what pastors learn from human experience, or else theological formulations are likely to be used in an unhealthy manner.

In the field of psychotherapy we can observe an intellectual approach very similar to that of Thurneysen, although different in content. Some psychotherapists, representing different schools, place great emphasis on the intellectual interpretation of a client's experiences in psychological terms. These therapists will place little emphasis on the feeling and meaning aspects of a patient's experience. The result is that the patient is likely to emerge from such therapy with a full indoctrination, fully committed to certain verbal formulations, but with problems still unresolved. Such patients can discuss human conflicts and problems, but they are very poor in their relationships with others. Fortunately, this seems to be true of a decreasing number of therapists. Our point here is that it makes little difference whether the content be psychological or theological, the result is very similar. Individuals find their security in a system of verbal formulations rather than in a growing ability to enter into human relationships through trust and love. They learn to live on the theories of others rather than on their own insights and understanding. According to Henry J. Cadbury, the method of Jesus was quite the opposite. He says,

> The kind of knowledge Jesus looked for was not so much imparted information as insight achieved. There is in fact reason to suppose that he did not refer so often to what his followers were to be told as to what they were to recognize and to discover.... Jesus' complaint is that men do not recognize the implications of their attitudes. But this is something you cannot simply tell them. It requires understanding, perception or insight.[5]

And we might add that such insight is fostered through a relationship of deep trust and acceptance.

Pastoral conversation, grounded in a relationship of acceptance and understanding in which the pastor becomes involved in the feelings and meanings of others, is aimed at enabling others to experience insight and understanding from within themselves. They learn to understand their actual relationship with themselves, with others, and with God, to discover the results of these relationships in terms of themselves and others, to find the questions raised by their situation and experience, and to discover for themselves their own answers in the light of the gospel. Real pastors do not have preconceived questions or answers. It is the experience of reality rather than acceptance of verbal formulations in which they are interested since such reality is the source of growth and fulfillment.

This seems to limit the formal use of theological concepts in pastoral care. Indeed, this is sometimes the case, depending upon the function that pastors are performing at the moment. Preaching and teaching are impossible without the use of theological concepts; in some other forms of pastoral care these concepts need not play such a prominent part. Indeed, in some instances pastors communicate only those concepts that would be healing or redemptive to the person immediately involved. But in all forms of pastoral care the concepts we offer will be empty and meaningless unless we are present with the person or group in the spirit of redemptive love.

The relationship of theology to pastoral care is recognized by theologian Carl Michalson. In *Faith for Personal Crises,* he says,

The theology which is being done in this volume is, I believe, what might be called a poimenical theology, a theology for the proper shepherding of sheep. (The Greek word, poimen, is the word for shepherd.) Restricting the scope of the treatment to the personal crises in the lives of the people, it is simply one branch of the care of souls. I have called that branch a theology for crucial situations. Unlike the traditional forms of theology, such as Biblical, historical and dogmatic theology, it does not need to say everything there is to say about the faith. It says only what is immediately pertinent to the situations at hand. It may even deliberately soft pedal some elements in the total body of belief which might obstruct the healing process. It has the aim of relieving rather than intensifying the crisis. It will not deal in magnitudes of knowledge, for what is needed in a crucial situation is not true propositions but an understanding of one's life. Nor will it become authoritarian and directive, insisting on the truth of its claims. There is just no point to that. Under conditions of crisis the truth must validate itself, entering as a liberating perspective. There is only one test of truth within a crucial situation: Does it illuminate and heal? Even that test cannot be applied before the therapeutic process has set in.[6]

Pastoral care should not be limited to events of crisis, but should see its tasks also in terms of the processes of growth, of being and becoming. However, we believe that the point made by Michalson is equally applicable to the broader concept, especially to certain expressions of it. Verbal formulations have their value, but they are powerless to create the experience to which they strive to give rational form. Such experiences are generated out of the potentialities of being when one person is associated with another in a relationship of self-giving love. When there is a trusting response to such love, a person is created or healed. The major difference between becoming ourselves through growth and becoming ourselves through healing in a moment of crisis is that in the first experience nothing has to be undone and re-done. As pastors we should be as much concerned with this means of growth as with healing in crises.

The communication of the gospel is therefore something more than the communication of verbal or logical concepts about the gospel. The gospel is concerned with the person as *being,* as being before God, as being created and called into existence by God. The gospel is concerned with the redemption of human beings through the restoration of the lost Image of God in which we were created. This redemption means calling human beings into fulfillment, into our full measure of being. Such an experience reaches far deeper than the verbal and logical capacities of the human being. It reaches into those nonrational aspects of being out of which comes the power for being or the dread of being. It is on this level that we experience ourselves as persons before God, or as broken, guilt-laden, anxious individuals seeking to escape from both ourselves and God. It is this level of being that responds in trust to grace and love, that experiences a sense of inner certainty, that senses meaning in personal relationships and responds accordingly. Ideas alone do not promote growth or healing on this level. Here ideas become real and elicit their appropriate responses only through the reality of relationships. John Calvin, in spite of his emphasis on intellectual formulations, has written,

> For the Word of God is not received by faith if it floats on the surface of the brain; but when it has taken deep root in the heart, so as to become an impregnable fortress to sustain and repel temptation. But if it be that the right apprehension of the mind proceeds from the illumination of

the Spirit, his energy is far more conspicuous in such confirmation of the heart ... the furnishing of the heart with
assurance being more difficult than the communication of
knowledge to the understanding.[7]

Genuine assurance arises from the nonrational, emotional depth
of being and is authenticated by the spirit of trust and love.
But there is a pseudo assurance prevalent that is a compulsive
acceptance of verbal ideas without genuine inner authentication
in being. Only in the quality of relationship that we have been
describing can the creative and healing work of the Holy Spirit
be manifest.

Pastoral Care and Pastoral Activities

Pastoral care, the communication of the gospel to persons at
their point of need primarily through relationships, should be
distinguished from the activities through which it may be carried out. Preaching, religious education, church administration,
calling, counseling, conducting worship, and other activities of
the pastor are forms of pastoral care. But if these forms are
engaged in by the pastor without a relationship of love and concern for persons, then they lead to ineffectiveness and disillu-
sionment for both pastor and people. Actual harm may result
when the pastor is too strongly motivated by negative feelings
toward persons. Pastoral care, the participation of pastor and
people in experiences through which the gospel of redemption
becomes real, must be genuinely motivated, or it is nothing.
Furthermore, the work of the Holy Spirit through the pastor
is not necessarily confined to the present forms. Perhaps in today's world we need some new forms through which redemptive
participation can take place.

In recent years, at least one old form has been revived, that
of hearing confessions, now referred to as pastoral counseling.
The revival of this form has frightened many people for various reasons. Yet confession is inherent in the gospel and in
the biblical witness, and there is profound need for it in human experience. It is a form of pastoral care that the church
must foster and develop far beyond its present scope, or we
must surrender an essential ministry aimed at the deeper levels

of human need to the so-called secular priests of healing. This will drive many who feel called to the ministry of healing out of the pastoral ministry, and lose others from the church. The church should rather develop the practice of pastoral counseling to the full, carefully delineating its values and limitations and the kind of training it requires. Pastoral counseling and professional psychotherapy should exist as two independent but cooperative professions, with deeper understanding developed between the representatives of both professions.

Pastoral counseling should not be identified with pastoral care, but this is one of the many forms of pastoral care. Counseling is a process by which a person communicates to the pastor on the level of deep personal feelings in order to work out or resolve a personal problem. When the need for counseling is at an end, the deeper aspects of the relationship of pastor and person are relinquished, since the pastor's responsibility is to help others resolve their dependence on the pastor and become responsible toward God. Just what this means concretely depends on the needs of each person. All pastoral counseling ought to involve pastoral care, but not all pastoral care is carried on through counseling.

Pastoral care, as we are interpreting it, is more than a ministry to persons in crises. It is also a ministry to persons at the point of growth. This is in sharp contrast to previous concepts of pastoral care. Many human crises are unnecessary and could be prevented by proper care before the situation reaches critical dimensions; many could be forestalled by experiences that promote growth. On the other hand, not all human crises are preventable, since there are elements in the human situation that cannot be predicted or controlled. The deepest need of a human being is for relationships in which growth may take place. The kind of personal decision and commitment for which the Christian faith asks cannot be given unless a certain level of maturity has been reached. The experience of decision may be a crisis, and growth will be both a contributing factor to, and result of, its true resolution.

We have been describing pastoral care as a quality of relationship that should find expression in various pastoral activities. In considering pastoral activities more specifically, we shall be limited by the fact that elaboration of the point of view of this book on each of these activities would require a book in itself.

Preaching is a form of pastoral care; that is, it is a means through which the pastor attempts to speak to a congregation in terms of the meaning of the gospel for human need. To say that preaching is proclamation is to state only half of the truth. The proclamation must be brought into dynamic relation to human need, or else we have only a dissertation on theology. As a dissertation it may be theologically acceptable, but also it may be completely meaningless to the congregation. Effective communication of the gospel in preaching requires that preachers speak out of a genuine experience of themselves before God and before others, in which they have learned the meaning of self-giving love.

Preaching is indeed communication and is always a two-way process. Preachers who speak out of their theological knowledge alone will find themselves engaging in a one-way declamation contest. The people cannot respond because they have not participated in theological study. But the gospel asks for much more than an intellectual response; it demands a response of faith that involves the whole person. If people are to respond, if there is to be conversation, their needs must be involved in the process of communication.

The gospel is communicated in preaching only when the ideas and concepts of the sermon find a reality in the experience of both speaker and hearer. Thus the preacher may speak of the love of God while many in the congregation are thinking, "I can't believe that God really loves me. I wish I could believe this." These persons may feel this way because they did not know a genuine human love in childhood. For similar reasons some persons may accept the preacher's words superficially, but find no deep response to them. They may enjoy the sermon because it feeds their fantasy of being loved. Or the preacher may speak of trust, faith, forgiveness, or another theme, with the same result. Ideas and concepts are interpretations of the gospel, and there is real communication only when the hearer and speaker experience the reality to which the ideas point.

Consider the preacher. Preachers may speak of the love of God with anger in their voice, and if so, they communicate anger. Preachers can speak of the forgiveness of God in a manner that leaves the congregation feeling more guilty, or reveals the preacher's own guilt. Preachers may speak of faith and communicate their own anxiety. Or they may speak "with the tongues of men and of angels, but...." It is rather amazing that through the centuries of preaching, much of it ineffective, preachers have been on the defensive rather than predisposed to discover the roots of the problem. One form of defense has been the idealization of preaching through books and lectures. Another has been the kind of theological interpretation of preaching that places all the responsibility for effective communication on God or the Holy Spirit. While we would not minimize the Word of God or the work of the Holy Spirit, we are insisting that the quality of the relationship that the pastor creates with the people is one of the profound sources of effectiveness or ineffectiveness in preaching. The pastor's relationship blocks or provides a context for the work of the Spirit. Theological education needs to ponder the significance of this in terms of methodology in teaching young men and women to preach. We need to place less emphasis on courses dealing with the mechanics of preaching and stress much more the approaches that will promote the growth of the preacher as a person.

Likewise, the gospel may be embodied and portrayed in the institutional form that is the church, but institutional forms are not the gospel. The church may be interpreted as the "Body of Christ" with so much attention given to the structural organization and program that the redemptive relationship is lost. The gospel is a living reality that creates and sustains the institution, and that in turn may create and re-create persons through the medium of the institution. If the administrative functions of the church are not used for their deeper pastoral purposes, they will be used for ends that are destructive of persons. The creative life of the minister is at stake in the same issue!

Again, the gospel is much deeper than an abstract ethical ideal or the mores or cultural pattern of a particular community. Certainly, ethical ideals are involved in the life of any Christian, and many of the problems brought to the pastor will involve a conflict of ideals or a failure to meet ideals. However, the essence of the gospel is not in an abstract description of human behavior, but lies in the deeper motivation from which the behavior springs. This is the meaning of Paul's insistence that love is the fulfillment of the law and of the statement of Jesus that he came not to destroy the law but to fulfill it. A moral code never produced the fruits of the Spirit. It is possible unconsciously to commit spiritual suicide by doing the right acts for the wrong reasons. A mother may feed her infant in an attitude of genuine love, or she may do it in an attitude of pseudo love that covers up a deep rejection of the child. In each case the child will be fed, but the effect on the child will be the difference between healthy and neurotic growth. The preaching of ideals rather than the mediation of love may be an expression of our own unconscious guilt. Tragically, we have known this to be the case.

Again, the ritual and liturgy of worship are forms through which the relationship of the gospel may be very effectively communicated in depth, or the attention of the priest and the worshipers may be kept on the surface. Ritual is composed of words, but also of acts through which the deep, inner meaning of the gospel is portrayed. The task of the priest before the altar is to represent God to the people, and the people before God, and thus to act in the role of a mediator. The call "Lift up your hearts," used in so many services, may fall on ears deadened by external and internal pressures, so that no lifting up is possible. The result is emptiness and meaninglessness. Words and acts are present, but not the inner reality of the experience of worship. The deepest act of Christian worship occurs in the Holy Communion, where, through the concrete acts of eating and drinking, something of the Spirit of Christ and the meaning of his life may be taken into the worshiper. Such a service may be a profound ministry of pastoral care, but many persons will first need another form of pastoral care — that of confession or counseling — in order to work through the inner barriers to the kind of response that the Communion asks. Thus one form of pastoral care may be dependent on another and vice versa.

With some psychological and theological insight, the pastor may discover that overemphasis on form, be it rational, institutional, liturgical, or ethical, is in itself a kind of personality perversion and a kind of idolatry. Its aim is to protect the person from inner reality and truth that would provoke strong anxiety. As Jesus himself pointed out, and as confirmed in any textbook on abnormal psychology, form is very appealing as a substitute for inner reality. Religious forms may be used for concealment rather than for insight, especially when the content concerns the deeper, nonrational aspects of the person. The deepest communication of the gospel is on the level of relationship that portrays and illuminates the Incarnation. Vital communication uses forms, but only for the purpose of mediating an inner spirit.

In Chapter 1, I spoke of the disintegrating forces at work in the daily experience of the pastor. The integrating factor in the work of the pastor is not to be found in forms or activities as such, but in the reality of the gospel that should be communicated to persons through those activities. Insofar as forms or activities serve other purposes — institutional, moralistic, or indoctrinational, for example — this deeper, integrating factor will not be present.

Having mentioned the Holy Communion, a word is in order in regard to the sacraments as the medium of communication of some aspect or quality of the grace of God. In addition to the theological understanding of the sacraments, pastors must understand the psychological processes that condition or determine response of persons to them. Pastors may observe situations of greatly overdetermined response that grow out of compulsive needs within a person or a group. An illustration of this is Luther's use of the confessional.[8] We have known Protestants to participate compulsively and ritualistically in the Holy Communion when they do not have the resource of the confessional. On the other hand, psychological factors may block a positive response to a sacrament, or create a strongly negative response. Pastors will learn about some of these factors if they make this the subject of conversation when they call on those parishioners who systematically avoid the Holy Communion. At other times, participation in the Holy Communion may bring into focus serious problems of the participants, so that they seek out the pastor for help. We have known many persons whose emotional problems blocked any vital experience in worship, but in whom worship became a vital and living experience after they had found the resolution of their problem through a counseling relationship with the pastor. The counseling experience, essentially one of confession, can become a sacrament even though it may not be officially and theologically recognized as such.

Throughout this book we have been interpreting the sacra-

mental nature of human relationships when they are lived within
the context of the gospel. It is essential to perform the sacramental rites that grow out of, and remind the worshiper of, experiences in the life of Jesus. But Jesus himself found in human
relationships, and also in natural processes and events, meanings that communicated some truth about the Kingdom of God.
And to Jesus, words themselves had a sacramental value — "the
words that I have spoken to you are spirit and life" (John 6:63).
Human relationships and the words that formulate and convey
their meaning can communicate the deep realities of the Christian faith when these realities are present in experience, and only
then. At such times relationships become sacramental. A cup of
cold water given in genuine concern and respect for the recipient — that is, given in the spirit of Christ — portrays something
of the grace of God. Genuine pastoral care is a constantly sacramental relationship.

Speaking and Hearing as One Process

So much of the work of the pastor involves verbal communication that some further technical comments on speaking and
hearing are in order. The ear is a receptive organ. Hearing
means taking in words, ideas, feelings, and making some response to them. Words may be accepted and remembered without a grasp of the meaning the words convey. One sees this
in the student who has memorized theological or psychological
words and can repeat them in speech or in writing, but who becomes confused and lost when asked to state what they mean
or to use them meaningfully. It is possible to hear and accept
an idea in verbal form while remaining unaware of or rejecting
the content. We really understand a communication only to the
extent that we are emotionally ready to grasp it. We hear what
we want to hear, and often we do not hear the real communication. Perception of the outside world, either through seeing
or hearing, follows patterns of the personality. This is especially
true of the perception of relationships. Our perceptions are distorted by our own needs and defenses. Jesus understood that
many had ears but could not hear in the deeper sense.

A great deal of hearing is negative. We have to say "No"
before we can say "Yes," like the man in the parable of Jesus

(Matt. 21:28–31). Our defenses are constantly operating, even though we are not aware of it. Indeed, we so identify our real self with our defensive processes that we spring to the defense of our defenses. Thus a student in a class in theology or psychology may reject an idea because it creates anxiety in her. Instead of examining her anxiety, she springs to the defense of her denial by becoming hostile to the teacher who presented the idea. Later when her anxiety subsides, she may wonder why she reacted so violently against the teacher, since she now hears the same idea in an altogether different way.

The process of identification is important in the speaker-hearer relationship — in the effectiveness of speaking and in the accuracy of hearing. Unless people feel that the pastor is with them deeply, they will feel that what the pastor says is beside the point. How many times one hears a person say, "He just doesn't understand me," or "She doesn't know what I am going through," or "He is not concerned with me, but only with his own ideas." The speaker, being the one who has taken the initiative, will demonstrate an understanding or lack of understanding of the hearer. The hearer is very likely to respond in kind whether positively or negatively. (Or at least try to.) People need to feel understood, and then they tend to identify consciously or unconsciously with the speaker. A student may identify with a teacher because he sees something in the teacher that is like one of his parents. Such identification may be either positive or negative, but the "hearing" of the student will be affected by these conditions.[9] Likewise, individuals in a congregation may reject the message because they cannot accept the messenger. Or they may reject the messenger because they cannot hear and understand the message. In all forms of pastoral care the pastor and the kind of relationship the pastor actually creates with others are controlling factors.

Hearing is also affected by the fact that the spoken word may "cue off" or stimulate responses within the hearer. Sometimes it is not the word itself, but the tone of voice or inflection with which it is spoken. The same word spoken maliciously or in jest or seriously will cue off different responses. These responses are also related to the individual's previous experiences and their meanings. Thus our response to the phrase "God is our heavenly father" may be either negative or positive, depending on

our feelings about our earthly father and how we have handled
these feelings, and also depending on the nature of our fantasies
about heaven. Many words used in religious speech can cue
off association in human relationships. Meanings developed in
human relationships in early childhood may be associated with
religious expressions in adult life, either positively or negatively.
A person may find it impossible to accept or even to understand certain religious ideas because these ideas set off negative
feelings based on our previous experiences. One student in a
certain course found himself going to sleep when certain ideas
that created intense hostility in him were expressed. He liter-
ally put himself out of hearing. Another student exposed to the
same ideas will react with excitement and want to plunge into
a heated discussion. The same words and ideas produce quite
different responses because of the way in which they are heard,
and this in turn is determined by meanings growing out of previous experiences. There is a great difference between that kind
of religious education that teaches religious words and ideas,
and the kind that aims at helping persons to understand the
meaning of their relationships with others and with God and to
find appropriate words in which to formulate and communicate
their ideas. The basis for a real community of spirit is not only
the use of words in common, but more deeply the experience of
common meanings.[10]

In the light of what we have been saying, we should look
again at the insistence often heard today that "faith comes from
what is heard, and what is heard comes by the preaching of
Christ" (Rom. 10:17). There is certainly a literal truth in this
statement. In the light of our discussion, two comments are in
order. First, the preaching of Christ by a person who is anxious
and guilt-laden, or who confuses faith with sentimental dependence and submissiveness, or who confuses Christ with creedal
statements about Christ, will hardly produce a vital faith. Only
the preacher whose own faith is genuine, and who is able to
meet the people in self-giving love, will be able to preach in
the manner that inspires living faith. Second, the hearers either must have experienced previously or feel at the moment of
hearing something of the reality in relationships for which Christ
stands. It is not only the intellectual content of the sermon that
is crucial, but the relationship that exists between speaker and

hearer as well. There needs to be a measure of unity between this content and the quality of relationship. The statement of Paul is often interpreted in a mechanical manner that misses these deeper aspects of communication of the gospel. So much preaching does not inspire faith because words and reality are not one, and Christ is not preached authentically.

So much has been written about the pastor as a listener that more may seem superfluous. However, pastors will not be able to speak to the depths of another person until they have learned to listen to their own deeper feelings and meanings. They must listen below the level of the manifest content of speech. Also, pastors will not be able to listen to others more deeply than they have listened to themselves. It is in listening to ourselves and others that we may hear what Thurneysen repeatedly calls "the Word of God." This phrase as I use it here does not stand for some preformulated idea, but rather the reality of the person-to-person and person-to-God relationship as it is revealed in the crux of experience. Even while pastors are preaching, they must learn to observe the responses of the congregation — according to facial expression, restlessness or attentiveness, the manner in which the congregation is listening. Such sensitivity can make it possible for pastors to respond in terms of the needs of persons as these are being communicated at the moment, often unconsciously. Dependence on a written manuscript or on too full an outline can seriously interfere with this dynamic process in preaching. Speaking and hearing is a total process in which the relationship of speaker and hearer is deeply involved.

Speaking and hearing, then, are really one process. As one hears, one speaks. Speech reveals the speaker, and sometimes discloses profound defensiveness, concealment, and lack of insight. In extreme form, speech can become psychotic delusion or hallucination. Or speech may grow out of a profound openness to oneself and the meanings of one's experiences, and then it becomes sharing. Such speech does not aim at manipulating; it aims at self-giving. But one cannot give until one discovers what it is one has to give. To be able to verbalize the meanings of one's experience is to have first received those meanings into consciousness, to become aware of them, to know oneself directly rather than to know about oneself. Speech that carries insight born of self-discovery has the possibility of communicat-

ing insight to others who are able to hear. Becoming a pastor is a matter of growth, of being and becoming, of openness to self and to others, rather than of learning the right verbal formula or how to say the correct thing. The frequent question of pastors, What do you say to persons in such-and-such a situation? should be changed to, What can I be to persons in such a situation?

Personal Obstacles to the Pastoral Relationship

We need to look at the pastor's personal obstacles to nonverbal, deeply personal communication in any aspect of the pastoral ministry. Such involvement with persons is actually very difficult for many pastors because of the nature of their own human relationships in the periods of growth from infancy to adulthood. Pastors are not of a different breed from other people, but possess the same needs, partake of the same kind of experience, and have the same kind of problems. In childhood a pastor may have been hurt by someone who loved her or she may have been rebuffed when she endeavored to give love to others. If so, the pastor may experience anxiety and perhaps guilt when she attempts to give love to her parishioners. Because the pastor has been hurt she may have built defensive barriers around herself to keep people at arm's length, dealing with them intellectually but not relating to them as persons, observing their sufferings from an aloof position but not participating or sharing in their sufferings in any deep sense. Many pastors with this unconscious attitude find encouragement in their theological training — if they have the "right" theology, can speak the right formulas, and quote the right authorities, then they feel they can discharge their responsibilities.

Our theological schools, which now place heavy and justifiable emphasis on intellectual training, should also accept their responsibility for helping students to become pastors in a deeper sense by creating opportunities for emotional and spiritual growth comparable to the intellectual training. But many pastors, because of a feeling of incompetence in the deeper levels of human relationships, react negatively to the idea that they can communicate the reality of the gospel only by participating in the deepest sufferings of others in self-giving love. For in not having received at the point of their own deep needs, they have not learned to give. Or they may confuse superficial and sentimental acceptance of the idea with the authentic experience. When we hear students or pastors say, "All I have to do is to love people," we know we are in the presence of persons who are willing to accept the idea verbally as long as they do not have to take responsibility for inquiring what this means for them personally. Such pastors are not to be condemned: they need a rich experience of pastoral care, and in some cases deep psychotherapy, before they will be able to give a genuine love. Until this occurs they will not be able to participate in the sufferings of others. This is one reason why some pastors espouse the theory that says that all the preacher has to do is to "proclaim the Word" and leave the rest to God — a very comfortable doctrine for those who are threatened by personal involvement. The Word indeed needs to be proclaimed, but its deeper content can be communicated only by one who is deeply involved both in the Word and in the predicament of human beings.

There is another reason why communication in depth is difficult for many to understand. We have participated in a culture that tends to ignore if not deny the inner meaning of human relationships, and to stress utilitarian rather than personal values. We manipulate persons as things, and use them for our own ends. This culture is dominated by utilitarian, money-making patterns, in which persons are valued according to what they produce rather than as persons. Such a culture creates individuals who find it very difficult to understand and accept the personal values implicit in an incarnational religion.

Another cultural situation operates against understanding on the personal level. Our culture is dominated by science, and science deals with a level of reality that can be described effectively by means of verbal symbols. The truth of science is not affected by the personal attitudes of the communicator. But the pastor is communicating an order of reality entirely different from that of the scientist. To describe and communicate facts about objects or observable or measurable processes is quite different from communicating our personal meanings in relation to other persons, or to God. It is for this reason that many scientists have rejected religious truth or reality; they are so committed to their own plane of comprehension and method of communication that they reject other levels of reality and the language appropriate to those levels of reality.. The temptation of the pastor has been in the other direction: to seek to compete with science by developing religious ideas into almost a "scientific system" to be communicated verbally. But the very nature of religious reality makes such exact verbal formulation impossible.

Still another reason why the idea of communication through relationships is hard for some to understand is our tendency to overintellectualize emotional and spiritual problems. By this we mean the attempt to formulate our emotional and spiritual problems in intellectual terms, then to formulate an answer that is usually the reverse statement of the problem (e.g., the answer to fear is faith), and then to seek to "apply" the answer to ourselves. This leads to the repression of dynamic aspects of the self, and thus to unhealthy results. Sometimes counselors discover the extent to which individuals have confined themselves to a rigid intellectual system, but more importantly they uncover how that system is being used to repress the deep emotional elements that created the problem they are trying to solve. For example, adherence to a rigid intellectual system and its promulgation may be an attempt to solve the problem of insecurity. The problem is only concealed by a false sense of security accompanied by a compulsive need to justify oneself by convincing others of the truth of the system. Feelings of insecurity can be adequately dealt with only by working them through at their roots. The tendency to overintellectualize becomes extreme in some persons suffering from a schizophrenic illness, but most of us have sufficient inner conflict to find this false solution appealing.

This tendency is very strong in modern culture and in the modern church. If we only have the right formulations we can solve all problems, so we feel. For the pastor, this may mean having the "right theology" without sufficient regard for the deeper dimensions of "personhood" or Christian experience. Philip Watson, in his book *The Concept of Grace,* points out that the sacraments of the church stand guard against the overintellectualization of the gospel.[11] Many persons need the kind of relationship with a pastor that enables them to penetrate beneath their overintellectualizations. They fail to respond to the sacraments for the same reason that they need to overintellectualize: they cannot allow another person, human or divine, to get through to a part of themselves that they feel compelled to exclude even from their own consciousness. It is very painful if another touches a part of us we cannot accept in ourselves.

Pastoral Care and Judgment

Our interpretation of pastoral care may seem to leave open the question of judgment. We can say frankly that we see no place in pastoral care for the passing of judgment in terms of condemnation or name-calling, or of moralistic preachments. Judgment is the prerogative of God, not of human beings, and pastors who easily assume the responsibility of speaking for God in a condemnatory manner had better look into their own motives. We should understand that as we judge, so are we judged.

On the other hand, the need for judgment, in another meaning of the word, is inherent in life. As persons we are constantly in need of a sense of where we are, what we are, who we are, and where we are going. At times we need to face or be faced with the significance and consequences of our attitudes and actions. Every serious student of human life knows that all persons have within themselves forces and patterns that are destructive and those that are creative. Part of what it means to be human is that persons may become aware of, and exercise some direction of, these forces within themselves. We do not experience this kind of awareness of the meaning of our own life by drawing into ourselves. We find it by evaluating or understanding ourselves in the light of another person with whom we are in a redemptive relationship. At times another person may need to speak the word that brings us to our senses, that breaks through our blind spots. But this word must be spoken in love, not in condemnation. A genuinely loving person can be angry and at the same time understanding. As a pastoral caregiver, there may be times when I am angry at something destructive that I see people doing to themselves or to others, but I must speak to them through love, and even then failure may result.

All of us at times need the experience of self-evaluation in the light of another person with whom we are in a redemptive relationship. At the moment of judgment, when we become aware of our guilt, we need also to become aware of the reality of God's forgiveness, and of the alternatives of accepting or rejecting this forgiveness. When we reject the love offered by another we are not judging that person; we are really judging ourselves as unworthy of that love or incapable of accepting it. Any feeling of guilt or sense of worthlessness is an act of self-judgment, but always in the light of an image of what we should be or desire to be. At times this image comes from others. However, the deepest guilt we can experience is the consciousness that we have not found our essential self. Out of our own guilt we may hurt others in order to bring punishment on ourselves or to justify self-punishment; but there is no redemption in this. The real need is to discover the truth about ourselves, which can happen only in relation to another who accepts us as we are, both guilty and forgiven.

The Christian understanding is that judgment belongs to God, not to human beings, that God does not pronounce judgment for its own sake, but that it serves the purpose of God's redemptive love. This judgment is not spoken primarily in words, but in the consequences of our being what we are, the consequences of our feelings, attitudes, actions. Because we have often refused to accept the principle of psychological determinism, we have blinded ourselves to the fundamental cause-and-effect relationship that God has written into human life, while at the same time we exercise moralistic judgments that are often false and inadequate because they are based on externals. The task of the pastor is very frequently that of helping people read the judgment that God is writing of their daily experience and being, in the very consequences of their acts and relationships. It is easy to thunder from the pulpit that whatsoever we sow that shall we also reap, but it is quite another thing to help persons come to understand the significance of this in their own being. Judgment is part of the communication of the gospel, but it is the judgment of God, not of the pastor, and the task of the pastor is to mediate this judgment by helping persons discover what is happening to them in their own experience. And this process will proceed from person to pastor, not in the reverse, as the pastor meets the person in redemptive love. This is part of what it means to communicate the gospel to persons at the point of their need; to help them discover their need, and simultaneously to bring them a relationship through which they can move to find the answer. Pastoral care is helping persons see all sides of their existence and its meaning, their potential for creative as well as destructive forms of being and becoming, and enabling them to choose in the light of the consequences. The will of God is not to be known so much through mystical intuition as through the consequences of our daily choices.

One other aspect of judgment should be mentioned here. Pastors stand under the same judgment as do the persons to whom they are attempting to communicate the gospel. There is the demand that pastors take the beam out of their own eye so that they may see more clearly to take the mote out of the brother or sister's eye. Pastoral insight into others will come best through their insights into themselves; it is this acceptance of their own true humanity that should keep pastors genuinely humble. Their own struggles and problems should lead them to resources that will be of great value in helping others.

All persons, including pastors, stand in need of discovering the reality of their own being and the meaning of their own existence. This reality has both its creative and its destructive aspects. To be confronted with negative aspects of oneself without at the same moment becoming aware of creative resources is a seriously traumatic experience. True pastors are those who have found the reality of their own being before God, who are aware of the destructive possibilities within their own nature, and who have brought these under some measure of subjection to the creative forces of their being through the grace of God. They are therefore persons of deep hope and courage, and face others in hope and courage. Thus their love, reverence, and trust of others calls from them the potentials of their being.

This is the matrix of the authority of the pastor as it was of Jesus' authority. People knew they were in the presence of a true human being when they faced him because his relationship with them carried its own authenticity and validity. In this way he mediated the love of God to them, and also a sense of what it means to be a true human being. The creeds tried to express this by the phrase "very God of very God and very man of very man." The true authority of pastors rests on the same basis. Their genuineness finds its own self-validation in the lives of those to whom they minister. This will be the pastors only authority in helping them to discover the reality of their own being, and to judge themselves in the light of the Person of Christ.

The redemptive love of which we speak is the affirmation of others as persons and as children of God, a deep intention to help others find the fulfillment of the potential that God has created in them, and the willingness to meet others at the point of their deepest need, which will mean in their suffering.

Such communication of the gospel through a relationship of love is described by Brunner in the following words:

> In love I will the other person to be as he is, that is as God gives him to be, and yet at the same time I will him to be different, as God wishes him to be. But since, before all else, God wills that I should be different, since before all else, I must remember that by nature I oppose my will to that of the other, the first and also the surest sign of genuine love is my acceptance of the other person, the attitude which does not correct him, or "pull him up" or demand or resist. The distinctive mark of the Christian ethos... is positive love, self-sacrificing surrender, which from the psychological point of view is the highest activity.[12]

Judgment needs to be related to acceptance. Acceptance involves and includes judgment. Acceptance is a relationship freely offered to others because they are persons, and because the giver is able to respect them as persons. Judgment is a necessary evaluation of the behavior of the person. It is the acceptance of facts about the person. If a man is a murderer, he should be accepted as a person who has committed a murder. Acceptance does not mean blinking at facts or realities; there is no cure or salvation in this. Cure or salvation will come only in an accepting relationship in which self-judgment and evaluation are encouraged through the pastor's ability to know the worst there is to know and still accept the other as a person deserving of understanding. In rare instances this understanding may be communicated in anger (Matt. 21:12; 23:1–36).

On the other hand, to demand acceptance from others is an expression of narcissism. Some persons demand the privilege of doing as they please regardless of the rights or needs of others, or without any legitimate social control, and of still being, in their own words, "accepted." But they are not really asking for acceptance; they are asking for indulgence. They want others —

God, and the world — to be an indulgent parent while they are permitted to play the role of the infant. Acceptance in social relationships, or in a community, involves the rights and needs of others, and persons who demand indulgence deny these rights and needs. In a pastoral relationship the pastor must be prepared for demands for indulgence. If they are tolerated here — and sometimes they are — it is for the purpose of helping the person gain insight and make necessary changes in behavior.

Sometimes, instead of demanding acceptance, persons will demand judgment from the pastor. In these instances they may be expressing a need to be punished or a need to be deeply dependent. These needs are both childish and unhealthy, and for the pastor to fall into the trap presented by such persons is to do them harm. But acceptance of these persons does not mean that we have to fall into this trap. It means that we accept them as persons, but as persons who have particular needs, and where possible we seek to help them understand and work through these tendencies. Again, there is a kind of judgment here, not in the sense of condemnation but in the sense of evaluation and helping another to make self-evaluation. Acceptance does not mean that we are to treat all others as they want us to treat them; to do this to some persons would be to reinforce their position and to encourage them to continue in some neurotic pattern — in short, to hurt them.

In describing the task of the pastor as the mediation of the love of God we are obviously stressing the central characteristic of God as seen in the Christian revelation, the Parenthood of God. God as Father/Mother not only creates and sustains us, but seeks our redemption and fulfillment. But there is another aspect of the nature of God that is related to growth and to judgment, and that is the Lordship of God in Christ. The Lordship of God may be interpreted childishly in terms of an authoritarian, punishing attitude, or in terms of a more mature acceptance of responsibility for oneself before a God who is acknowledged as the ultimate authority in personal life. Tillich has pointed out that the Lordship and Fatherhood of God need to be kept in constant tension in order to avoid making God into either a demonic power or a sentimental old man.[13] The tendency to overemphasize one of these qualities in God at the expense of the other is not of a logical origin; it is rooted in a personal need for punishment or in a childish dependence and need for protection. Either bias leads to a neurotic kind of person and religion. On the other hand, a dynamic tension may be hard to maintain. This requires a certain level of emotional maturity. In the final analysis pastors' own sense of the Lordship of Christ, or of the ultimate authority of God in the choices and decisions of daily life, will be communicated to those to whom they minister. It is important that pastors understand through their own experience that the Lordship of Christ is a necessary accompaniment of the redeeming love of God. In all human experience there is nothing so inexorable and demanding as love, and nothing that brings suffering into human life as does the lack of love. Christ could not have revealed the redeeming love of God without at the same time revealing the Lordship of God.

NOTES

1. Eduard Thurneysen, *A Theology of Pastoral Care* (Richmond: John Knox Press, 1962), p. 15.

2. Ibid., p. 109.

3. Ibid., p. 107.

4. Martin Buber, *Between Man and Man* (New York: Macmillan Company, 1947); Reuel L. Howe, *The Miracle of Dialogue* (New York: Seabury Press, 1963).

5. Henry J. Cadbury, *Jesus, What Manner of Man?* (New York: Macmillan Company, 1947), pp. 94–95.

6. Carl Michalson, *Faith for Personal Crises* (New York: Charles Scribner's Sons, 1958), pp. 12–13.

7. John Calvin, *Institutes of the Christian Religion,* 6th ed. (Philadelphia: Presbyterian Board of Education, 1813), bk. 3, chap. 2, p. 526.

8. Erik Erikson, *Young Man Luther* (New York: W. W. Norton, 1958), chap. 5.

9. Some readers will recognize that we are speaking here of a kind of experience described by psychoanalysts as "transference." For further study of transference see Carl Menninger, *Theory of Psychoanalytic Technique* (New York: Basic Books, 1958), chap. 4.

10. For further discussion of words as cues see John Dollard and Neal E. Miller, *Personality and Psychotherapy* (New York: McGraw-Hill, 1950), pp. 106–109.

11. Philip Watson, *The Concept of Grace* (London: Epworth Press, 1959), p. 27.

12. Emil Brunner, *The Divine Imperative,* trans. Olive Wyon (Philadelphia: Westminster Press, 1947), p. 328.

13. Paul Tillich, *Systematic Theology,* vol. 1 (Chicago: University of Chicago Press, 1951), p. 286.

$\prec$ **5** $\succ$

*Pastoral Care and
the Growth of Persons*

I N A PREVIOUS CHAPTER we referred to the traditional approach in pastoral care, that is, to the work of the pastor in dealing with the natural crises of life. Discussions of pastoral care have centered on such events as birth, marriage, illness, death.[1] This approach has had certain values, not the least of which is that at times of intense suffering from events in our common experience some persons are more open to a pastoral ministry that at other times.

But this approach also has its limitations. As we have indicated earlier, the way in which people meet one of these universal crises is closely related to the level of emotional growth they have achieved at the time, since the meaning of an event is determined quite as much, if not more, by what a person brings to it, as by the event itself. Furthermore, many crises are produced by the failure of persons to grow emotionally.[2]

The idea of growth is not foreign to the Christian faith. Such concepts as "growth in grace" and "going on to perfection" are ample indication of this. But the Christian faith has not produced a workable theory of personal growth. This is not said in criticism, but rather in delineation of a task; for such a theory of growth is a psychological, not a theological, problem, although it has many theological implications. Throughout the history of pastoral care, current psychological theories have been utilized by pastors in their work.[3] This is one indication that some such theory is a necessary background for vital involvement with persons, which otherwise might deteriorate into a relationship controlled by the pastor's own prejudices and fantasies.

Creative pastoral involvement, then, requires some understanding of what is going on within persons, that is, the processes by which they have become the persons they are. However, the conceptual formulation of such processes must always be hypothetical, subject to revision and reformulation, and never considered as "ultimate truth."

Much of the criticism that the pastoral care movement is too much involved with Freudian theories has been the result of misunderstanding.[4] Some of these criticisms, however, have been based on a sound insight that might be stated thus: How can an adequate theory of pastoral care and its involvement with persons utilize a psychology that stresses the development and control of instinctual drives? Actually some advocates of the Freudian point of view in pastoral care have wrestled with this problem much more than have the critics, for they have been in a position to be conscious of its significance. But insofar as they were also familiar with the biblical account, they have understood that many of the Freudian concepts, particularly Eros and Thanatos, are amply illustrated in biblical material, always with an additional religious dimension.[5]

Any pastoral or religious understanding of the human being must give full consideration to the problem of instinctive human drives as these are expressed in daily experience, as well as to the problem of cultural opportunities and deprivations in the satisfaction of these drives. The Christian faith has sought to play a vital role in the "internalization" of the external authority of the culture through what Freud called the "superego"; the Ten Commandments are an excellent example of this. However, the Christian faith has also been interested in the human soul. In recent decades the word "soul" has suffered from misuse, and the word "self" has tended to replace it. Christian thinkers, however, have recognized an aspect of the human person that is not adequately formulated in the concepts of either instinctive drives or superego. Theologically speaking, this aspect is the soul or spirit; psychologically, it is the self or the ego.

Some Freudian analysts also have become aware of a dimension in persons that was not sufficiently elaborated in Freud's theory, and they have set about correcting this weakness. We refer to the development of ego psychology in recent psychoanalytic thought.[6] The work of Erik Erikson on ego development is of particular significance for pastoral care.[7] Erikson, a psychoanalyst and a specialist in child therapy, has also approached the problem of growth from the point of view of cultural anthropology. He is concerned not only with what is going on within individuals, but also with what individuals mean to their culture and their culture means to them, and what these meanings may contribute to the process of ego development. Because of our conviction of the value of Erikson's approach for pastoral care, we shall outline his basic concepts. It should be kept in mind, however, that this discussion is not much more than an outline, the purpose of which is to encourage the reader to wrestle with Erikson's own works. We are not presenting his ideas as "ultimate truth," which indeed he would not do either, but rather as a stimulating and fruitful approach to some of the problems of ego development that are vital to pastoral care.

Here we need to speak frankly of two dangers to be avoided in considering Erikson's work. One is the tendency to try to turn ideas into a program. Pastors who have not been adequately trained in pastoral care, or who may have personal problems that lead them to emphasize programs rather than personal relationships, or who have been overencouraged to organized activities by superiors, often overemphasize programs and the programming of ideas. Nothing could be further from the spirit of Erikson's work or from the essence of pastoral care! Repeatedly we will be saying that the basis for ego development is in human relationships, not in programs. Programs may furnish an opportunity for relationships and the communication of meanings through relationships, but programs in themselves may be used as a deadly substitute for deeper realities.

The other danger is the conversion of concepts of ego development into "oughts," that is, into ethical imperatives to be preached or a rigid system to be promulgated. To be sure, there is something of an ethical imperative implied in personality development itself. The person must grow, in ego, in conscience, and in impulses, or the person becomes sick. But growth takes place through personal relationships, not through ethical preachments or legal systems. For example, Erikson speaks of infancy as the stage in which the basic conflict is between trust and mistrust.[8] Trust in infancy may become the foundation for all trusting relationships throughout life, and we would add, for religious faith. Preachers are always looking for ways of reinforcing their insistence that persons have faith; but we need to see that faith, like trust in infancy, is not the product of exhortation or of being told that one should trust. Real trust grows out of relationships with a person or persons who are trustworthy and who show it in their daily contacts. So it is with all the other qualities of ego growth. The task of the pastor is not to tell persons how they ought to grow, but rather to help them by creating conditions and relationships within the church that make growth possible. Therefore, our purpose here is to increase the understanding of pastors in their relationships, rather than to assist them directly in programming or peaching. But pastors can be very sure that when they talk about faith in the pulpit their own trust or lack of trust will be felt by the congregation!

As a background to understanding Erikson, it is desirable to have a familiarity with the general theory developed by Freud: the concepts of the id, ego, and superego; the problem of anxiety, repression, and ego defenses; and the psychosexual stages of development. This approach is discussed helpfully in other works to which the reader is referred.[9]

The work of Erikson centers on understanding the ego and its development. The ego may be pictured as midway between the id and the superego. The word "ego" stands for those processes within the person that have the constant task of synthesizing inner needs and conflicts with the demands, frustrations, and values presented by other persons and the prevailing culture. In infancy, the ego processes are just beginning to develop, and may be very weak in relation to frustrations imposed by the environment, such as the withdrawal of love for whatever reason. Therefore, the ego may be subjected to problems of synthesis or integration for which it does not have the necessary strength. But it does have at its disposal certain "ego defenses,"[10] that is, psychological processes by which it can allay its anxiety and find substitute ways for the gratification of its needs. An ego defense is a substitute way of coping with a problem that cannot be directly mastered. One such defense is fantasy.

The ego has at its disposal in its synthesizing efforts the normal processes of perception, memory, imagination, reason, and motility. Defense mechanisms distort these normal processes in various ways. Says Erikson, "The ego, then, is an 'inner institution' evolved to safeguard that order within individuals on which all outer order depends. It is not 'the individual,' nor his individuality, although it is indispensable to it."[11] While the superego is the internal process by which the prohibitions and demands of the culture operate within the psyche, the ego reflects the personal meaning that individuals experience in relation to those about them. In different ways, then, both the superego and the ego represent internal processes through which the culture and its values become part of a person.

Emphasis should be placed on the word "processes." Psychological terms such as "ego" and "superego" are constructs — a kind of shorthand language for the way in which constellations of dynamic processes are organized for purposes of thought and communication. Thus when we speak of the "ego" we do not have in mind a definite locale in the psyche, nor an objective "thing." We do have in mind constellations of processes that become organized into a psychic structure through which the functioning of the person is carried out — in the psychic realm, as in the organic, structure and function are but different aspects of life processes.

The process of developing an identity begins in infancy and continues throughout life (it is the crucial problem of adolescence). Says Erikson,

> The growing child must derive a vitalizing sense of reality from the awareness that his individual way of mastering experience (his ego synthesis) is a successful variant of a group identity and is in accord with its space-time and life plan.... The conscious feeling of having a *personal identity* is based on two simultaneous observations: the immediate perception of one's selfsameness and continuity in time; and the simultaneous perception of the fact that others recognize one's sameness and continuity.... Ego identity concerns more than the mere fact of existence, as conveyed by personal identity; it is the ego quality of this existence.[12]

Identity, then, is related to the synthesizing functions of the ego.

But it is also related to the values and meanings of the group. It thus becomes a focal point for a vital expression of our relationship to our culture. The simultaneous perceptions involved in identity — recognizing our own selfsameness and continuity in time and realizing that others recognize in us these same qualities — speaks of the relationship that we have with others in our culture. A sense of identity arises out of perception of common meanings — within the self and within the culture. Lack of identity means conflict — we do not value ourselves as we perceive our culture valuing us or disvaluing us. There is a sense then in which the ego and its identity are our sense of our own value to ourselves and to others, our acceptance or nonacceptance, our being good or evil. Says Erikson, "the young individual must learn to be most himself where he means most to others — those others, to be sure, who have come to mean most to him. The term identity expresses such a mutual relation in that it connotes both a persistent sameness within oneself (selfsameness) and a persistent sharing of some kind of essential character with others."[13]

The sense of identity is related to the mechanism of identification. Through identification, children take into themselves characteristics of persons who influence them strongly either positively or negatively. But these separate identifications offer no unity; indeed they can become the basis of conflict when the children try to pattern themselves after conflicting identifications. We have known, for example, a young man whose vocational identifications with different persons led him both toward the ministry and toward medicine. He finally tried to solve his problem by becoming a hospital chaplain! But this was a projection of a fantasy, and not a real identity, since at the time he made his decision he had no real idea of what a hospital chaplain was. A sense of identity is formed as we sort out our childhood identifications, retaining some, rejecting others, but in the final decision, putting the stamp of our own individuality on, and making our own unique organization of, the outcome, which is our own identity. As Erikson points out, society *"identifies the young individual,* recognizing him as somebody who had to become the way he is, and who, being the way he is, is taken for granted."[14] He goes on to say that in forming an identity, the individual asks for recognition by the community, which the community is very happy to give; but it may react with hostility if the offer is rejected. The classical illustration of this is the persecution of heretics by the church! Identity is in part the gift of the group — a cultural process communicated through relationships. This is at least a part of the psychological meaning of the rituals of baptism and confirmation.

Our identity — or our failure to find an identity and therefore our lostness — is rooted in our historical-cultural traditions. The illness of the individual may reflect the illness of the culture, and may in turn be reflected in the culture. Erikson has three works on this theme of the relation of the individual ego and history.[15] His study of Luther not only reveals the conflict of the culture within the man Luther, but also the manner in which historical-cultural change and individual pathology are tied up with theological and religious ideas and practices. In this scrutiny, religion does not always emerge on the side of goodness!

This brings us to a problem as deep in human experience as it is in the Christian faith. In forming a sense of identity the individual has to sort out the evil from the good, and hopefully discard the evil. However experience has proved that this is no simple matter. Society and the church usually hold the individual responsible for this selection, not recognizing that in many and subtle ways society or the group itself has had a powerful hand in the selection. The struggle between good and evil is a problem for every human being, but in the emotionally sick person it becomes intensified. As Erikson indicates, there is an unconscious evil identity — that which the ego is most afraid to resemble.[16] This identity is made up of images that have been disturbing to the ego. The ego does not separate these memories nor discriminate between them, but lumps them together as bad or sinful under some symbol of evil.

Erikson indicates that in our society the unconscious evil identity is usually composed of images of (1) the violated body (a reference to the Freudian castration fear), (2) the ethnic outgroup, and (3) the exploited minority.[17] This seems to explain why ethnic outgroups and exploited minorities are often labeled as sexual perverts of one kind or another — all three "evil" images have become associated within the ego. He also points out the "sad truth that in any system based on suppression, exclusion, and exploitation, the suppressed, excluded, and exploited unconsciously believe in the evil image which they are made to represent by those who are dominant."[18] In this regard he has some unusually poignant remarks on the identity of American blacks that should be read by all concerned with the present racial struggle — and by those who are not yet concerned! It can be seen from this brief summary that Erikson has moved beyond the strictly individualistic approach of traditional psychoanalysis, although his work is rooted in that discipline. His concept of ego identity, in which individuals are related to the historical-cultural processes of which they are a part, presents many fruitful leads for the pastor or the interpreter of religion.

Erikson is as much, if not more, concerned with the growth of the healthy personality as he is with pathological development. In his formulations of growth he uses the epigenetic principle of biology as an analogy: "Somewhat generalized, this principle states that anything that grows has a *ground plan,* and that out of this ground plan the *parts* arise, each part having its *time* of special ascendancy, until all parts have arisen to form a *functioning whole.*"[19] This means that personality is not entirely the result of its social environment: the growing persons bring to experiences of social interaction potentialities of their own that emerge in a certain time-growth sequence, and "the healthy child, given a reasonable amount of guidance, can be trusted to obey inner laws of development, laws which create a *succession of potentialities for significant interaction* with those who tend him."[20] For example, the first ego potentiality in infancy is trust. If trust is not learned in infancy, it becomes more difficult or, under some circumstances, impossible to learn later in life. Furthermore, it becomes the basis on which positive ego qualities develop after infancy. But these qualities exist as undeveloped potentials before the stage in which they receive critical development. Thus the autonomy that characterizes the second stage of ego growth is present in some undeveloped form in earlier infancy.

No ego quality, such as trust, emerges without crisis or conflict. Thus the child may and does experience in infancy relationships that create mistrust. Erikson speaks of this conflict as a "decisive encounter" with the social environment. Other persons communicate to the infant their particular feelings and meanings for the infant, and these are positive or negative, good or evil. Thus "each stage becomes a crisis because incipient growth and awareness in a significant part function goes together with a shift in instinctual energy and yet causes specific vulnerability in that part."[21] Shifts in instinctual energy are usually reflected in changes in behavior, interests, and goals. Thus in certain respects children may have consolidated their strengths, while in others they may seem weak and uncertain. When this occurs they are especially vulnerable, and other persons react in various ways to their sense of weakness. It may be a signal for some to do too much for children rather than encouraging them to do for themselves. At least there will be a response, a fact which leads Erikson to write, "A family can bring up a baby only by being brought up by him. His growth consists of a series of challenges to them to serve his newly developing potentialities for social interaction."[22]

Thus each successive step in growth "is a potential crisis because of a radical *change in perspective.*"[23] But the crises of growth, when they become serious, are also crises in the relationships between the child and "significant others" when mutual regulation has broken down.

The concept of mutual regulation is in direct contrast with the principle of relationships that operates in many homes, that is, control of one another. It is not always the parent who controls the child; the child may control the parent. Erikson sees the needs of child and parents as complementary: the child needs a relationship of nurturing trust and autonomy, and the parents, if they are emotionally healthy persons, need to give such nurture. Thus there is a reciprocity of need. When the individuals in a family are controlling themselves in a manner appropriate to age and status, mutual regulation results.

The patterns of mutual regulation change as the child grows and the parent matures. Such patterns cannot successfully be developed artificially or by precept, since they really consist of the subtle but powerful interactions of persons with each other and are often motivated below the level of consciousness. Any pattern of relationships that depends on exploitation, domination, or possessiveness destroys mutuality. What are usually taken as "behavior problems" in children may be symptomatic of a breakdown of mutuality between parent and child. It would seem then that energy spent in attempts to teach children the difference between good and evil would be used to better advantage in helping them to understand themselves in their relationships with others, particularly the ways in which their own attitudes and actions are destructive.

Basic Trust versus Basic Mistrust

The first crisis in ego development is characterized by Erikson as that of trust or mistrust. This occurs in the first year of life, when the capacity for trust emerges from within the child and seeks a response in the mother. In calling such attitudes "basic," Erikson means that they pervade both the surface and the depth of the personality, that is, they are part of conscious experience and ways of behaving, and are also unconscious inner states. He regards "basic trust as the cornerstone of a healthy personality."[24]

The impairment of basic trust in infancy is experienced as a sense of mistrust. Mistrust, which is a form of anxiety, makes it impossible for the individual to find comfortable relations with others or with self.

The crisis of trust or mistrust — the emergence of the need and its answer or frustration by those caring for the infant — is related to feeding in this "incorporative stage," when not only are children receptive to food, but also to emotional satisfaction, comfort, and a sense of well being, that is, a sense of being given to as they need. As Erikson says, the infant "lives through and loves with his mouth; and the mother lives through, and loves with, her breasts."[25] The attitudes of the mother toward herself as a woman and a mother, and toward her child, are important ingredients in her effort to provide emotional as well as physical nourishment. Here is an illustration of "mutual regulation" between the individual and another person. "The mutuality of relaxation thus developed is of prime importance for the first experience of friendly otherness: from psychoanalysis one receives the impression that in thus *getting what is given,* and in learning to *get somebody to do* for him what he wishes to have done, the baby also develops the necessary groundwork to get to be the giver, to 'identify' with her."[26] The sense of trust developed in this relationship becomes the basis for a sense of identity in children, a feeling that they have meaning and worth both to themselves and to others.

But frustration is inevitable, and Erikson sees the crisis coming during the second part of the first year, when there is an increase of physiological tension owing to teething and other changes, when infants are able to distinguish themselves from other objects and are becoming aware of themselves as persons, and when the mother is likely to turn away from the infant in favor of other activities. There is a certain leeway in what may happen to a child in terms of frustration. Erikson is clear that it is not frustration in itself that is damaging, but the failure to communicate meaning to the child. "Parents must not only have certain ways of guiding by prohibition and permission; they must also be able to represent to the child a deep, an almost somatic conviction that there is a meaning to what they are doing."[27]

Out of the crisis of the oral stage, where experiences of trust or mistrust are crucial, arises a deep sense of loss. "Our clinical work indicates that this point in the individual's early history provides him with some sense of basic loss, leaving the general impression that once upon a time one's unity with a maternal matrix was destroyed."[28] This loss is usually related to weaning — perhaps breast feeding was abruptly withdrawn when the infant began biting — and to a general loss by the infant of the mother's attention and presence as other demands are made upon her time and energy. The sense of loss may be such as to create acute infantile depression or a mild, chronic state of mourning that can affect the rest of a person's life.

> But even under more favorable circumstances, this stage seems to introduce into the psychic life a sense of division and a dim but universal nostalgia for a lost paradise. It is against the combination of these impressions of having been deprived, of having been divided, and of having been abandoned, all of which leave a residue of basic mistrust, that basic trust must be established and maintained.[29]

Obviously, no infant arrives at the end of the first year without some experiences that create mistrust, but it is to be hoped that the infant has had enough experiences that inspire trust to outweigh them. Erikson is clear on the need to establish enduring patterns for the balance of basic trust over mistrust. This is first of all a task for maternal care, and it "does not seem to depend on absolute *quantities of food or demonstrations of love,* but rather on the *quality* of the maternal relationship."[30]

Erikson describes trust using almost the same terms as for identity, indicating that trust is a fundamental ingredient in the sense of identity:

> The general state of trust...implies not only that one has learned to rely on the sameness and continuity of the outer providers but also that one may trust oneself and the capacity of one's own organs to cope with urges; that one is able to consider oneself trustworthy enough so that the providers will not need to be on guard or to leave.[31]

In words current in theological circles today, trust is essential to the development of a sense of community; infants must experience a safe and satisfying relationship with others, through which they gain emotional strength to cope with problems presented to them both by their world and from within themselves.

On the relation of trust to religion, Erikson has some significant comments. He is concerned with whether or not in any given group "religion and tradition are living psychological forces creating the kind of faith and conviction which permeates a parent's personality and thus reinforces the child's basic trust in the world's trustworthiness."[32] He draws analogies between much that religion promises and the context of infancy, such as the need to be provided for and to trust in a provider. Also, "All religions have in common...the insight that individual trust must become a common faith, individual mistrust a commonly formulated evil." He concludes: "Whosoever says he has religion must derive a faith from it which is transmitted to infants in the form of basic trust; whosoever claims that he does not need religion must derive such basic faith from elsewhere."[33] For an intensely stimulating and illuminating discussion of the conflict of trust and mistrust in a religious genius, the reader is referred to Erikson's *Young Man Luther.*

Autonomy or Shame and Doubt

The second crisis of ego development, beginning in the second year, centers on another organ and its functioning. In classical Freudian language, this is the anal stage. According to Erikson, the process of toilet training provides opportunities for mutual self-regulation that can have a far-reaching influence on the development of the ego. He sees the basic crisis here as between autonomy on the one hand and shame and doubt on the other.

The psychosocial modalities of this stage are retention and elimination — "holding on" and "letting go." Hoarding things or throwing things away is expressed not only in toilet training, but in many activities of children. Indeed, if the adults cooperate, children will make a game out of this with their toys, which can perhaps be carried over to their toilet experiences. For the first time they are being asked to learn to control their muscular structure, and this requires learning an inner control. Children at this stage are often described as "having a mind of their own," that is, they show an emerging capacity for autonomy, for making the decision for retention or elimination, holding on or letting go.

Erikson sees this stage as a severe test for the mutual regulation between mothers and children. If maternal control is too early or too rigid, it destroys the opportunity for children to learn to control their functions and activities by their own free choice, and this leads to a sense of defeat and rebellion.

> This stage, therefore, becomes decisive for the ratio between love and hate, for that between cooperation and willfulness, and for that between the freedom of self-expression and its suppression. From a sense of *self-control without loss of self-esteem* comes a lasting sense of autonomy and pride; from a sense of muscular and anal impotence, of loss of self-control, and of parental overcontrol comes a lasting sense of doubt and shame.[34]

The development of autonomy rests on a continuation of the earlier sense of trust. Out of such trust, combined with firm treatment, children will sense that what is being asked of them has meaning for them, and they will feel some protection from their own strong urges.

The alternative to autonomy, a sense of inner decision in making one's movements, is shame and doubt, which reflect a sense of helpless exposure that one would like to escape, and a real question as to one's value as a person. What Erikson calls the modalities of "holding on" and "letting go" can find either positive or destructive expression toward society or toward the self. One negative result in children is the development of the tendency to "overmanipulate themselves," to develop a "precocious conscience." Such persons become the classical "compulsive" characters — repetitive, stingy, needing to hold on rather than let go, and needing to control. Or they may become the kind of persons who, failing in any genuine autonomy, put on a show of autonomy in an overcompensatory way.

Erikson sums up his advice to parents of children at this stage: "Be firm and tolerant with the child at this stage, and he will be firm and tolerant with himself. He will feel pride in being an autonomous person; he will grant autonomy to others; and now and again he will even let himself get away with something."[35] He warns that there is no substitute for genuine autonomy in the parents themselves, just as there is no substitute for their genuine trustworthiness. "When it comes to human values, nobody knows how to fabricate or manage the fabrication of the genuine article.... For no matter what we do in detail, the child will feel primarily what we live by, what makes us loving, cooperative, and firm beings, and what makes us hateful, anxious, and divided in ourselves."[36] Erikson's stress on values as communicated through relationships, and on the corollary of this, that parents, teachers, and pastors cannot give what they do not have, is shared by many who are engaged in helping others.

Initiative versus Guilt

If children have successfully resolved the conflict of autonomy versus shame and doubt, which is characteristic of the second year of life, they will be ready to face the next ego crisis, that of initiative versus guilt. They have already shown the capacity to try to get what they want; now, and in a special way, the impulse to be "self-activated" emerges as a dominant quality. Successful resolution of the previous conflicts becomes the basis for growth at this stage.

The stage of life from three to about six or seven is known in Freudian terms as the period of the Oedipus and the Electra complex — the period in which the boy has feelings of a sexual nature toward his mother and a sense of resentment toward his father, who seems to stand in his way, and the girl has feelings of a sexual nature toward her father and a sense of resentment toward her mother, who seems to stand in her way. Erikson's work incorporates all of the stages of psychosexual development described by Freud, but he moves beyond the vicissitudes of the instinctive drive to the problem of ego development associated with a given period of the child's life.

Children at this stage are able to move about; their energy and curiosity propel and guide their movements. They are observant, inclined to ask questions endlessly, and they can understand in a childish manner the patterns and roles of adults in their environment. Now they are able to play with other children, and they learn from one another. "His learning now is eminently intrusive and vigorous: it leads away from his own limitations and into future possibilities."[37] The psychosocial mode of this stage then is intrusive, "intrusion into other bodies by physical attack; the intrusion into other people's ears and minds by aggressive talking; the intrusion into space by vigorous locomotion; the intrusion into the unknown by consuming curiosity."[38]

The sexual curiosity of this stage is focused on the sexual organs and their possible uses. Sexual play of various kinds with other children takes place. However, the wish of the child for sexual relationship with the parent of the opposite sex, and at the same time to take the place of the parent of the same sex, becomes the source of much fantasy, hostility, and guilt. In many ways the child is inadequate in comparison with the adult, but here the child is especially inadequate and subject to frustration. Consequently, a strong sense of guilt is likely to arise — "a strange sense, for it forever seems to imply that the individual has committed crimes and deeds which, after all, were not only not committed but also would have been biologically quite impossible."[39]

It is at this stage that conscience, "the great governor of initiative," becomes firmly established. "The child now feels not only ashamed when found out but also afraid of being found out. He now hears, as it were, God's voice without seeing God."[40]

Conscience can be oversevere, cruel, and inhibiting, and can burden children with so much guilt in regard to their sexual and hostile feelings that their initiative is blocked or seriously hampered in its expression. For example, the children's curiosity, not only about sexual matters but about all things, may be so seriously curtailed that they do not want to learn new things. The sense of guilt is likely to make children feel that they, rather than their behavior, are bad, and they may look for ways to prove that they are not. On the other hand, they may act badly in order to draw punishment and thus alleviate their guilt for a time. Erikson points out that one of the common forms of overcompensation for the feeling of being bad or worthless in our culture is finding a sense of worth in what we are doing or are going to do, rather than in what we are, with the consequent overdevelopment of drive toward activities.

The answer to this phase is continued mutual regulation of the life of children and adults. Again, there is no substitute for giving children genuine love and understanding, accepting their conflicts and problems, and doing things together with them in a way that helps them anticipate their someday becoming competent adults — competent in love and work. Erikson points out that there is no time when the individual is more ready to learn quickly to become "big in the sense of sharing obligation, discipline, and performance rather than power, in the sense of *making things, instead of 'making' people,* than during this period of his development. He is also eager and able to *make things together.*"[41] A sense of equality in worth is expressed in the companionship of parent and child, particularly when they are of the same sex. Children's feeling of sharing rather than a sense of being exploited on the basis of weakness or size will help them overcome their guilt, at least in a measure, and prevent it from becoming a crippling factor in their egos. They will retain initiative, guided by conscience, and by the values learned in the relationships they have experienced with their parents and other adults.

Industry and Inferiority

In the next period of growth, the classical "latency" period, no new drives emerge to be mastered. But it is a period of great social learning and ego development, and this is the aspect we are about to consider. Movement into the latency period, as with all periods, will not only mean that children face new tasks, but also that they will need to face and seek to resolve the emotional conflicts carried over from previous stages of growth. At this stage children want to learn how to do and make things both on their own and with others.

Now children are sent to school, and they begin the process of learning in a formal setting — through prescribed duties or more adventurously, according to the system. But children also like to play, and it is important at this time, for the benefit of their later life, for them to learn to work when they work and play when they play. Erikson points out, however, that play for the child is not recreation in the adult sense, but is often the child's "way of thinking over difficult experiences and of *restoring a sense of mastery.*" If the child's first play is properly handled by adults, "the *pleasure of mastering toy things* becomes associated with the *mastery of the conflicts* which were projected on them and with the *prestige* gained through such mastery." Since play at this age usually involves other children, and children are introduced into a world of sharing with their peers, play now becomes a means of learning to master experience by "mediating, experimenting, planning, and sharing."[42]

Children at this stage want to be useful, to be able to make things and to make them well. Erikson calls this the sense of industry. Skillful guidance at this stage is important; but if children's conflicts in previous stages have not been sufficiently resolved, they may not want to grow to be competent in doing and making. They will be content to let others do and make for them. This can create a sense of inadequacy and inferiority — a danger at this stage — that may continue into adult life.

Children derive a sense of their social value through their meaning to others as persons who can do something worthwhile. When, however, doing or making things becomes a matter of competition with others or a way of defeating others, activity is in part motivated by hostile feelings, and no sense of mastery or industry will result. According to Erikson, this is "socially a most decisive state: since industry involves doing things beside and with others, a first sense of *division of labor* and of *equality of opportunity* develops at this time."[43]

Identity versus Identity Diffusion

We have already dealt in a general way with the problem of ego identity. In adolescence achieving or maintaining a workable identity is the central problem. The sense of identity that has accrued up to this time may be disturbed because of new and quite radical physical growth and the emergence of sexual feelings and potentialities not hitherto experienced. At the same time society faces youth with problems of vocational commitment that are not unrelated to their sexual commitments. The task now before adolescents is to re-form their sense of identity, to find a new sense of continuity and sameness that others can accept. In order to do this, they may again have to face unresolved crises of earlier periods.

As indicated earlier, ego identity is the integration of the identifications that the young persons have previously made. But it is more than this, for they have brought to these identifications a selective process and also the stamp of their own individuality, so that the final synthesis is a unique identity.

The danger in adolescence is identity diffusion. Here young persons are unable to integrate their emerging forces with the positive or negative values of their childhood relationships and come to a sense of their meaning to their world. Erikson comments that "it is primarily the inability to settle on an occupational identity which disturbs young people," and that the intolerance of many adolescents is a "necessary *defense against a sense of identity diffusion.*"[44] However, there seems to be considerable identity conflict in youth today on the sexual level and also, as seen from within the pastoral ministry, on the religious level. Youths caught in a sense of identity diffusion not only cannot make decisions and move toward meaningful goals, but they also are at the mercy of their impulses as well as their conscience. Erikson says that "a gradually accruing ego identity is the only safeguard against the *anarchy of drives* as well as the *autocracy of conscience,* that is, the cruel overconscientiousness which is the inner residue in the adult of his past inequality in regard to his parent."[45]

Another concept related to the identity crisis is that of the moratorium. This is society's way of providing, and the youth's way of accepting, situations in which identity decisions may be postponed. Erikson refers to Luther's early years in the monastery as such a moratorium.[46] Certainly anyone dealing with students today can observe them using college, and even seminary, as a way of postponing the decision as to what they are to be. The frequency with which some students change their major fields of study, or their inability to make a decision as to future vocation, is using the moratorium in an attempt to solve the problem of identity diffusion.

Another concept significant in relation to the adolescent is that of a negative identity, "meaning an identity which he has been warned *not* to become, which he can become only with a divided heart, but which he nevertheless finds himself compelled to become, protesting his wholeheartedness."[47] Parents often have a way of realistically presenting to the child the very patterns they consider dangerous and undesirable. Sometimes, in order to solve an identity crisis, the youth chooses a negative identity. "Many a late adolescent, if faced with continuing diffusion, would rather *be nobody or somebody bad, or indeed, dead — and this totally, and by free choice — than be not-quite-somebody.*"[48]

Much has been written about the "storm and stress" of adolescence. This period, says Erikson,

is not an affliction but a *normative crisis,* i.e., a normal phase of increased conflict characterized by a seeming fluctuation in ego strength, and yet also by a high growth potential.... What under prejudiced scrutiny may appear to be the onset of a neurosis is often but an aggravated crisis which might prove to be self-liquidating and, in fact, contributive to the process of identity formation.[49]

From a research project of a university health service comes material supporting Erikson's concept of identity conflict and diffusion. This is a study of "an acute confusional state in college students." The authors consider this state to be "an emergency anxiety reaction to a combination of stressful conditions, where environmental insecurity is associated with internal conflicts of both shame and guilt in young adults of reasonably strong ego, who have suffered severe infantile trauma." The symptoms presented include (1) confusion, (2) inability to concentrate, (3) a feeling of helplessness, (4) a feeling of terrified isolation. With treatment the prognosis is good; without treatment it may be doubtful, and pathological conditions may result. The authors conclude:

> In childhood these patients were bound in an extraordinarily strong dependent relationship to their parents through guilt and fear, engendered by parental instability and disharmony. With subsequent dependent gratification and support these patients were able to achieve a conforming type of adjustment and to gain success in academic and social achievements. However, in young adulthood when they attempted to find their own identity, through choice of heterosexual partner and choice of career, in the college environment, devoid of dependent gratification, their previous adjustment was inadequate to meet their needs. Sexual temptation or commitment may lead to guilt, which may lead to retreat. Retreat, in turn, may lead to shame and ridicule from the peer group. To avoid the shame, another attempt at conforming sexual behavior may be attempted, and once more guilt, retreat and shame. In this way, either thrusts toward accomplishment or retreat from it are associated with anxiety. Under these circumstances, if the dependent gratification from parents is cut off, due to their criticism or disapproval, the patient regresses to an early childhood fixation point, associated with primary anxiety, rage, and confusion, where he feels isolated, worthless, mistrustful and depressed. Recovery may occur when the patient, who desperately seeks help, finds someone to lean upon. If no one is found to meet these needs, reaction formation to the rage (the wish to save mankind rather than destroy it), introjection or projection may result.[50]

Intimacy and Distantiation versus Self-absorption

We come now to the first stage of adult life, where the ego, if it has successfully resolved the crises of the previous stages, is inwardly ready for intimacy. Erikson is clear that sexual intimacy is only part of what he has in mind. Indeed, persons who are confused in their identity may enter into sexual relationship without experiencing intimacy. He is, rather, speaking of an "interpersonal intimacy," which includes the sexual but also a close emotional and social relationship of a deeply satisfying and mutual nature. One basic condition for intimacy is a firm sense of identity — "the condition of a true twoness is that one must first become oneself."[51]

"The counterpart of intimacy is distantiation: the readiness to repudiate, to isolate, and, if necessary, to destroy those forces and people whose essence seems dangerous to one's own."[52] On the other hand, because of the fear of loss of identity, a youth may avoid any kind of interpersonal relationships and move toward isolation and self-absorption. Distantiation, however, involves contact with others, albeit a manipulative, exploitive contact, while isolation means withdrawal, and if developed to an extreme form, becomes schizophrenia.

Erikson's description of mature sexuality ("genitality" in psychoanalytic language) has meaning for the experience of intimacy.

> The idea clearly is that the experience of the climactic mutuality of orgasm provides a supreme example of the mutual regulation of complicated patterns and in some way appeases the potential rages caused by the daily evidence of the oppositeness of male and female, of fact and fancy, of love and hate, of work and play. Satisfactory sex relations make sex less obsessive and sadistic control superfluous.[53]

Another way of saying this is that mutuality in sexual relations serves the purposes of emotional growth and well-being, but when mutuality is absent sex contributes to conflict and illness. But real mutuality in sex depends on a level of mutuality of being in which persons are open and self-revealing to each other in thoughts, feelings, and goals, and also in sexuality. The roots of many of the problems, and also of the joys, of marriage and family life will be found here.

Generativity versus Stagnation

The next stage of adulthood Erikson calls generativity, "because it concerns the establishment (by way of genitality and genes) of the next generation."[54] It is primarily the interest in establishing and guiding the next generation. As such, generativity is a stage of growth of the healthy personality, and "where such enrichment fails altogether, regression from generativity to an obsessive need for pseudo intimacy takes place, often with a pervading sense of stagnation and interpersonal impoverishment."[55]

The mature person needs to be needed quite as much as the offspring needs to be cared for. But some persons find it difficult to develop a concern for the nurture and guidance of the younger generation; they may produce children, but find the care of children difficult or burdensome because of their own immaturity. Erikson finds the reasons for such failure "in early childhood impressions; in faulty identifications with parents; in excessive self-love based on a too strenuously self-made personality; and finally (and here we return to the beginnings) in the lack of some faith, some 'belief in the species,' which would make a child appear to be a welcome trust of the community."[56]

Integrity versus Despair and Disgust

The final stage of growth is that of later maturity which, on the positive side, is characterized by Erikson as integrity, or "the acceptance of one's own and only life cycle and of the people who have become significant to it as something that had to be and that, by necessity, permitted of no substitutions."[57] This includes the resolution of ambivalences in regard to, and a new acceptance of, one's own parents; the acceptance of responsibility for one's own life; a sense of fellowship with all other persons, now and through history, who have communicated human dignity and love. Ego integrity "is the ego's accrued assurance of its proclivity for order and meaning. It is a post-narcissistic love of the human ego — not the self — as an experience which conveys some world order and spiritual sense, no matter how dearly paid for."[58]

One does not come to any final sense of ego integrity without having won a large measure of the positive values in each of the preceding stages of growth. On the other hand, failure to achieve a wholesome sense of integrity in the final stage brings a sense of despair and "an often unconscious fear of death: the one and only life cycle is not accepted as the ultimate of life."[59] However, time is short and it is impossible to start another life cycle in a belated attempt to find integrity. Such despair often shows itself as disgust with particular institutions or persons, a disgust that disguises the individual's contempt for self. "Ego integrity, therefore, implies an emotional integration which permits participation by followership as well as acceptance of responsibility of leadership."[60]

Comments and Questions

To develop all of the possible theological and pastoral implications of Erikson's thought is a task too large for the scope of any one book. His theories are profound and comprehensive, and are still developing.

Not all pastors will find the same meanings for their work in his interpretations, and this is as it should be. His work is especially significant for pastors because it places the inner world of individuals in a dynamic relationship to their cultural environment and human relationships. In doing this Erikson does not discard basic concepts of Freud, but he does elaborate the processes of ego development more fully. Also he has been able to see in the lives of his patients the meaning of their cultural environment to them and, in turn, their meaning in relation to their cultural environment. He is as concerned with the impact of personality on culture as he is with the impact of culture on personality. These two relationships cannot be separated.

Much of the work of the pastor falls in this area of the relationship between personality and culture. Any pastoral perspective that overemphasizes either approach to the exclusion of the other will not be effective. The social-gospel approach of the past generation suffered from this limitation. Pastoral counseling is sometimes characterized as a purely individual approach, with no social consequences. But pastoral counselors are aware of the impact of their work with one individual on a group of persons (a family), and of the impact of the group on one individual. And there is also a vocational perspective that is important for pastors, and that is whether pastors see themselves as teachers, reformers, preachers, or with some other function. In each of these the pastor needs to define goals in the light of personality-culture processes, if the pastor wants to utilize the forces that mold persons. Our theological orientation should contribute to this end. The goal for pastoral care, as we have been defining it in this book, is reconciliation, the resolution of conflict, the bringing together of the separated, the healing of both persons and society.

Erikson finds the answer to conflicts between individuals and between groups in the discovery of a more inclusive identity in which both sides may share and find a greater fulfillment. The pastor would understand the Christian faith as offering such an identity. It has been called variously the Kingdom of God, and the Christian community. But pastors must do more than preach these goals. They must learn new ways to participate as pastors in the conflicts of individuals and of groups in a relationship that leads to reconciliation or healing. This takes pastors directly into the life experience of their people, especially those experiences that most powerfully affect their existence. There is no area of human conflict foreign to the work of pastors. The creative processes of God are at work in all human relationships, and pastors should become the catalyst to help to bring these forces to fruition.

The study of Erikson will bring home to pastors a fact that we may have already gathered from other sources. We speak of the great importance of the first five or six years of life for the later development of the person. If the sense of basic trust, for example, is not developed in infancy, it may be exceedingly difficult if not impossible to develop later. If pastors reflect on the meaning of the developmental process as outlined by Erikson, they will become aware of the tremendous importance of pastoral care of the infant, the child, and the parents. If there is any one place where the emphasis of the church needs to be placed, it is with the parents of children under six years of age. This is not to minimize other stages of growth, but to stress the obvious fact that in infancy and early childhood significant beginnings in personal growth are made, or else they are not made. These beginnings center largely in the relationship of child and parent, in the feelings, values, and meanings they have for each other, and in how these are communicated. The relation of the parents to the larger group, and how that group evaluates parenthood and its responsibilities, is also important here. The problems of many adolescents and adults are basically the unresolved problems of early childhood, expressed in various distorted and symbolic ways. Growth needs to begin at the right time and the right place. Failure in growth at one stage makes the resolution of the crisis of the next stage very difficult. Basic ego qualities are best learned in their optimal stage.

Since it is necessary that any pastoral care of the small child be given through the parents, the pastor will stress the value of non-verbal communication of feelings and meaning through relationships. Even five- or six-year-old children may be struggling with feelings that are completely beyond their power to formulate in words — feelings of guilt, for example. Nor do they have to be told that they are forgiven or accepted. If the adults who are most significant to them really forgive and accept them, they will know it, and will not have to be told. In turn they will learn to be forgiving, even though they may not be able to verbalize it.

The fact that pastoral care of the child must be given through the parents deepens the responsibility of laypersons in the world, the world here being the home and family relationships. It is here in the home, in the early years of parenthood, that the husband and wife may learn some of the deepest realities of human relationship, and the child may actually become their teacher if they are able and willing to learn. For children are constantly saying something of importance to adults if we can see and hear and feel with them. This is an emotional kind of learning, and it may call for changed attitudes on the part of the parents. Through the nurture of the child the parents themselves may grow to be more genuine persons.

The child makes a continual contribution to the growth of the parent even as the parent nurtures the child. Erikson's principle of mutual self-regulation is sound; a similar principle is in Christian insight. In a sound approach to the pastoral care of the parents of young children, either in groups or individually, the pastor and parents alike would discover the forces that actually operate in parent-child relationships and the relation of these to the Christian faith. There is no area in which sound Christian insights are likely to have more meaning than here, and if they are not discovered to be meaningful here, there will be deep resistance to the discovery of their meaning in the larger community. If parents are helped in the spiritual nurture of each other and of their children, they will find it possible to respond in positive ways to the need of others outside their home — in the immediate neighborhood and in distant places. By giving more effective attention to the beginnings of the growth of persons, the church would have to give less attention later to problems such as alcoholism, divorce, delinquency, mental illness, and the like. But apparently we would rather try, and often fail, to pick up the pieces of broken humanity than to seek to prevent the brokenness in the first place. The major thrust of pastoral care should be at the point of growth. Experience has shown that if we stumble here we are also likely to stumble when we accept cure as our goal.

For those who would ask about methods of pastoral care of the family we suggest small group discussions where parents are permitted to express their feelings and concerns under the kind of leadership that helps them to work out their problems and achieve trust, autonomy, and other ego strengths within themselves. Along with this, some parents would ask for — and need — personal attention in pastoral counseling. Pastors need adequate training for both of these tasks. Also, we should be able to use other resources in the community.

Erikson as a scientist avoids theological and pastoral implications in his work, and rightly so. He offers us his insights into the nature of human growth, and it is up to theologians and pastors to bring to their work their own problems and insights, and to ask about relationships. This should be done, not just on the level of ideas, but with ideas that grow out of the close observation of life processes. Never in reading Erikson are we allowed to forget that he is a clinician, and that he is trying to state what he finds in his clinical practice. He is not just spinning theories. In method, too, he has something to teach the pastor.

The reader certainly has not failed to ask the significance of

Erikson's characterization of the first ego crisis as "basic trust or mistrust" for the Christian experience of faith. Basic trust is the beginning of ego growth, and a necessary element in each succeeding stage. The Christian faith insists that salvation is through faith, and faith is a person's self-committing response to the grace of God. What is the relation of the experience of basic trust in Erikson's meaning to faith in the Christian sense? To ask this question may seem to be heresy in some quarters, but it needs to be asked. One might make the further observation that the Christian faith often seems to be fixated on the idea of salvation through faith. Many Christian interpreters never seem to get beyond this particular formula. Is there nothing more to Christian experience? What is the relation, for example, of Christian faith to the ego crises of autonomy or initiative, or to the remaining crises — or to the negative aspects of these stages? Are Christian interpreters stressing faith as the beginning aspect of Christian experience, to the exclusion of other aspects that are important for the maturing ego? What would be the meaning of the much used phrase "growth in grace," in the light of ego development? Could it be that one reason for the lack of power so frequently discovered in the lives of Christians is the failure to relate their faith in a living way to their own processes of growth? Without in any way discounting or minimizing the importance of faith, theological correlations need to be made with the qualities of the maturing ego, and pastors should be trained to understand the relation between Christian growth and ego growth. One would hardly expect to find a creative, mature Christian experience in a person of childish or immature ego development.

Similar questions could be asked theologically and pastorally at each stage of development. At times preachers exhort their congregations to an interpretation of the Christian faith requiring submission to the will of God in a manner that would demand the surrender of autonomy. Some Christian hymns embody this idea. But it is becoming clear that the development of autonomy in early childhood is one of the marks of a strong person. To what extent do we unwittingly teach the identification of the will of God with pseudo-autonomous drives that would be unacceptable if seen as part of the self? On the other hand, is not a genuine exercise of autonomy essential to any deep and

creative Christian commitment? How can we give that of which
we have not yet come into possession? May not this be the reason for many "decisions" that fall by the wayside?

For many persons, cries of doubt continue throughout life.
Many great Christian leaders, such as Luther, were assailed by
strong doubts. When we reject a person's doubts we reject a living, though negative, aspect of a person's ego. In accepting and
understanding a person who has doubts, we help that person
to face, and either live with or resolve, the conflicts that lead
to doubt. Doubts about God cannot be separated from doubts
about oneself, and doubt is part of the experience of every person.

Genuine commitment, the commitment made in self-giving
love and trust, is not an act performed at a given moment, but a
basic quality of relationships that develops slowly, in little events
of life, beginning in early childhood.

Commitment is a response of trust, autonomy, and initiative
to day-by-day relationships that are trustworthy, permit freedom, and encourage concern for others. There is a time in late
adolescence when genuine commitment may become a matter of
conscious decision, but such a decision grows from within. It is
in adult life that the meaning of commitment becomes explicit
in many daily relationships. Here its genuine nature is attested
by spontaneity and warmth in ordinary relationships or conditions, and by deep courage and strength under stress. Pastoral
care given by genuinely committed persons — parents, pastors,
laity — is the climate in which deeply committed persons may
grow. But such persons will be committed to persons, values,
and relationships, rather than to institutions or creeds. And
therefore they will have a basis in their own being for understanding the meaning of commitment to Christ.

Many questions could be raised regarding the theological and
pastoral implications of Erikson's third ego crisis, initiative or
guilt. Consider the guilt experienced by young children because
they want something that is forbidden. Is this guilt before God?
We have known children of this age who were in terror about
what they had been told about God. These children apparently
related their guilt feelings, which are a normal part of this age,
to what they had been told about God. When, if ever, is guilt
developed in relationship to parents to be identified as guilt be-

fore God? And can the guilt feelings engendered at this early age
be more fully released through the symbolic forms of religion or
through a less symbolic process?

A further question is: What is the meaning of love in the life
of the child? Certainly the infant needs a kind of care that a five-
year-old would find objectionable, but at each age a kind of love
is needed that gives children a sense of belonging with those who
care for them, and that thus overcomes their sense of separation.
Children must have meaning to others, and others to them. The
stage of initiative is one in which children are learning to love
others in a way they have never experienced before. If they are
made to feel excessively guilty about this, or if sufficient trust
and autonomy have not accrued in the earlier years, they may
not have the strength to handle their guilt feelings constructively.
Or if the mother has been emotionally seductive to the male
child, an extra burden of anxiety and guilt is placed upon him.
Children learn what love means through the kind of love they
receive. From the depths of their being they want to love in the
sense of feeling a warmth, closeness, and unity with persons in
their surroundings.

The pastor and the church are committed to teach the way
of love. Christian love, as exemplified in Christ, is a self-giving
concerned with the needs of others, seeking no reward for itself,
and not only to refrain from harming others, but to creatively
contribute to their welfare and lead to a sense of community.
It seeks unity through a genuine concern and respect for other
persons that permits their freedom. Such love cannot be taught
by precepts. Children understand it when they experience it
from others and learn to be loving in return. But such love must
be specific; that is, it must be concerned with real needs; and real
needs may differ. Thus the love given an infant may be different
from that given a six-year-old. It is these differences that need
to be spelled out in the lives of parents and children, and this is
part of the task of pastoral care. Parents can accomplish much
of this themselves, if given freedom in small-group discussions.

But we in the church have often worked against ourselves.
We have taught the need for love, but we have made people feel
guilty about loving. We have done this through our attitudes
toward sex, transmitted from parents to children. Children who
are taught that their bodies are dirty and evil in the toilet train-

ing experience come to the stage of initiative with guilt already formed. When feelings relating to sex and love emerge, and especially if these feelings are rejected by the parents, more guilt is generated. Or if the new feelings receive too much acceptance and satisfaction from the parent, they may become threatening to the child. To cope with their guilt and anxiety children may withdraw their feelings from the parents. They lose initiative. They no longer can reach out for the satisfaction of their needs. And as they grow up they become adults who cannot love. This can create serious problems in the search for ego identity in adolescence or the search for intimacy in the young-adult period. They hear a sermon on love and devoutly wish that they could love, but feel inwardly blocked. Many of the problems of human relationships grow out of this situation. The church and the pastor need to examine their theology of sex and love, and particularly pastoral attitudes, to eliminate those elements that tend to create excessive and unrealistic guilt feelings in relation to love and sex, and to discover what needs to be done in our culture to help persons experience that form of love that is appropriate to their particular stage of life.

We used the phrase "excessive and unrealistic" in relation to guilt feelings in order to distinguish the constructive uses of guilt. For guilt and guilt feelings are not altogether evil. Like other aspects of life, they have a real purpose, which may become unhealthy when they are excessive or related to feelings rather than actions. But persons may be unhealthy also because they do not experience adequate and appropriate guilt feelings. They may have committed an act that is obviously harmful or destructive, but show no remorse. Indeed, persons may put on a front of good behavior in order to cover up their real values. Guilt in its healthy use becomes somewhat analogous to fever in the organism, an inner signal that something is wrong and needs to be corrected. As such, it is a part of every healthy person, since no one is perfect. But when guilt develops excessively, when it is used as a reason for self-punishment rather than self-change, or when guilt-producing structures are absent or do not function, then illness is in process. The Christian faith does not condone guilt. The forgiveness symbolized in the Cross requires change as part of the process of repentance and accepted forgiveness. Thus the Christian answer to guilt involves understanding, acceptance, and growth to a higher synthesis. Guilt is a signal for the need for growth.

By the time children have reached six, they have thoroughly experienced two profound aspects of life, good and evil. It could be hoped that the good might outbalance the evil in the life of every child, but this obviously is not so. From early infancy both good and evil have been mediated through the parents and other representatives of society — since no human being can be perfect. The church has been much concerned with the problem of good and evil, but all too often the concern has been expressed theologically rather than practically or pastorally. The child, and the adult as well, has a need to project evil into the world in personifications, such as the evil parent, teacher, foreigner, or representative of another race or class. In religion, evil has been personified as Satan or as a demonic spirit.

One of the tasks of pastoral care is to help individuals distinguish between real evil and supposed evil. Real evil, the truly demonic, is those attitudes, relationships, and actions that destroy oneself or others. Sometimes these may be clothed in the most righteous rationalizations. Supposed evil has numerous psychological roots, but there is a large element of narcissism in it. That which I do not want or which denies some of my desires seems to be evil. And it is usually necessary, for the sake of internal comfort, to project this evil on other persons or objects, often including God.

Another aspect of the pastoral task of helping persons distinguish between real and supposed evil is to enable persons to experience in relationship what the Bible describes as the love that overcomes evil. The biblical solution of the problem of evil is never repression or denial, but frank and open admission and honesty. This is always in the light of a forgiving, reconciling God, in whose love, experienced through human relationships, there is strength to overcome evil. Sometimes in childhood and in childish adults the law must be used to restrain the expression of evil. But the essence of the New Testament solution is that a person should grow up to the maturity that is in Christ, so that the control of evil is a spontaneous experience emerging from within, directed by the desire for reconciliation. And as Erikson's characterization of the stages of growth remind us, there is an evil aspect to each stage, and so the conflict between destructive and constructive forces may continue throughout life. This problem is never settled once and for all. It is constant and continuous, changing only in form. Its solution is in a deep personal identity that yields a constructive motivation through which evil is taken up into the good, and a new synthesis is created within the individual. The biblical injunction to overcome evil with good needs to be translated into the actualities of every stage of growth.

There are many other points at which questions of theological and pastoral correlation could be raised. One more comment will be ventured. Erikson goes to biology for the basis of his epigenetic principle of development, a principle that holds that there are present in the organism basic structures that at an optimal time will emerge if life conditions permit. Thus persons are not just the result of their experiences, but also of what they bring to those experiences in terms of emerging capacities. This is a corrective for that kind of psychology which sees a person as nothing more than a stimulus-and-response mechanism. But more important, there are theological correlations. For Christian theology has always held to something given in the nature of the human being. On the positive side this has been expressed in such symbols as "the image of God," and on the negative side as the human propensity to sin.

Sin has been interpreted as the failure to fulfill the potentials of the self in relationship to God. The presence of a structure within the human personality makes the fulfillment of the potentiality of that structure obligatory. The individual's inner being demands fruition, or else there is sin, destructiveness, and death. Reflection on Erikson's last stage of ego growth, that of final integrity or despair, in the light of a clinical knowledge of older persons, should help one understand the meaning of a basic structure in life, whether formulated biologically, psychologically, or theologically.

Christian theology has taken exception to a theory of the ego that holds that its primary purpose is adaptation to the world. Erikson's concept of ego development takes us beyond mere adaptation. The development of individual potentials is at stake. Furthermore, the individual ego has some power to change the world rather than adapt to it. One of the strong impulses of youth is to change the world, and this should be understood not only as a projection of young people's need to change themselves or as a sign of hostility, but also as an unarticulated insight that something in the world really needs to be changed. For there is something wrong in a society or group that fails to give youth the foundation for a viable sense of personal identity. There is such a thing as creative adaptation, which adapts to the environment by changing it. Pastors should recognize that persons will be likely to have a distorted view of, and relationship to, any ultimate or transcendent loyalties as long as there are serious problems of adaptation in the area of the proximate.

One of the tendencies in the church and the pastor is to become overly involved in symbolic content and functions and divorced from the real experiences of persons. Then we go on speaking in theological symbols that our people no longer seem to understand. We have had more than one voice raised lately over the meaninglessness of Christian theological symbols. But the answer is not necessarily in a new set of symbols. Symbols with actual meaning cannot be created by any artificial means, but grow out of dynamic experiences of individuals and groups, and then become reminders to future generations of those events.

Each generation must experience for itself not only the symbol but the reality and meaning in the symbol. In the task of mediating the gospel to persons, the pastor needs to be deeply concerned with the realities of the gospel and of human experience equally. Symbolic structure has creative meaning only when there is something in experience to be structured. Symbolism becomes an element in the formation of neurotic processes when symbol is divorced from inner experience and meaning and allowed to proliferate in a vacuum. This has happened in the past generation, and creative pastoral care is needed to bring vitality of meaning back into Christian experience.

NOTES

1. For the traditional approach to pastoral care see Paul E. Johnson, *Psychology of Pastoral Care* (Nashville: Abingdon Press, 1953); C. W. Brister, *Pastoral Care in the Church* (New York: Harper & Row, 1964); William A. Clebsch and Charles R. Jaekle, *Pastoral Care in Historical Perspective* (Englewood Cliffs, N.J.: Prentice-Hall, Inc., 1964).

2. This is amply illustrated by such books as Leontine Young, *Out of Wedlock* (New York: McGraw-Hill Book Co., 1954); Edrita Fried, *On Love and Sexuality* (New York: Grove Press, 1961); Dorothy W. Baruch, *One Little Boy* (New York: Julian Press, 1952).

3. Clebsch and Jaekle, *Pastoral Care in Historical Perspective.*

4. O. Hobart Mowrer, *The Crisis in Psychiatry and Religion* (Princeton: D. Van Nostrand, 1961).

5. Wayne Oates, *Religious Dimensions of Personality* (New York: Association Press, 1957).

6. See material on the work of Heinz Hartmann in chap. 3

7. Erik Erikson, *Childhood and Society,* 2nd ed. (New York: W. W. Norton, 1963); *Young Man Luther* (New York: W. W. Norton, 1958); Erikson, *Insight and Responsibility* (New York: W. W. Norton, 1964); Erikson, "Identity and the Life Cycle," selected papers with a historical introduction by David Rapaport, in *Psychological Issues,* vol. 1, no. 1 (New York: International Universities Press, Inc., 1959).

8. *Psychological Issues,* pp. 55–65.

9. O. Spurgeon English and Gerald H. Pearson, *Emotional Problems of Living,* 3rd ed. (New York: W. W. Norton, 1963); Ruth L. Munroe, *Schools of Psychoanalytic Thought* (New York: Dryden Press, 1955); Calvin S. Hall and Gardner Lindzey, *Theories of Personality* (New York: John Wiley & Sons, 1957).

10. Anna Freud, *The Ego and Mechanisms of Defense* (New York: International Universities Press, 1946).

11. *Childhood and Society,* p. 194.

12. *Psychological Issues,* pp. 22–23

13. Ibid., p. 102.

14. Ibid., p. 113.

15. *Psychological Issues, Young Man Luther,* and *Insight and Responsibility.*

16. *Psychological Issues,* p. 30.

17. Ibid.

18. Ibid., p. 31.

19. Ibid., p. 52.

20. Ibid.

21. Ibid., pp. 53–55

22. Ibid., p. 55.

23. Ibid.

24. Ibid., p. 56.

25. Ibid., p. 57.

26. Ibid., p. 58.

27. Ibid., p. 63.

28. Ibid., p. 60.

29. Ibid., pp. 60–61.

30. Ibid., p. 63.
31. Ibid., p. 61.
32. Ibid., p. 64.
33. Ibid., p. 65.
34. Ibid., p. 68.
35. Ibid., p. 70.
36. Ibid., p. 71.
37. Ibid., p. 76.
38. Ibid.
39. Ibid., p. 79.
40. Ibid., p. 80.
41. Ibid., p. 81.
42. Ibid., pp. 84–86.
43. Ibid., p. 88.
44. Ibid., p. 92.
45. Ibid., p. 93.
46. *Young Man Luther,* p. 43.
47. Ibid., p. 102.
48. *Psychological Issues,* p. 132.
49. Ibid., p. 116.
50. Helen B. Carlson, M.D., Carl Christensen, M.D., Alfred Flarsheim, M.D., Bernard L. Greene, M.D., William Nolan, M.D., Erich Paschkes, M.D., Charles Schlageter, M.D., Julian Pathman, Ph.D., and Clara Weimer, Ph.D., "Diagnosis and Treatment of an Acute Confusional State in College Students," in *Quarterly Bulletin,* Northwestern University Medical School, Chicago, vol. 32, no. 1, 1958, p. 6.
51. *Psychological Issues,* p. 95.
52. Ibid., p. 96.
53. Ibid.
54. Ibid., p. 97.
55. Ibid.
56. Ibid.
57. Ibid., p. 98.
58. *Childhood and Society,* p. 268.
59. *Psychological Issues,* p. 98.
60. Ibid., p. 99.

≺ 6 ≻

The Making of a Pastor

This CHAPTER IS NOT TO BE a discussion of the whole of theological education, but only of certain aspects that seem pertinent to the theme we have been developing.

A vital and creative Christian experience in the making of a pastor is clearly essential. The fact that many students enter seminary without such experience should not be held against them, but should be seen as a challenge to the school. Many of these students have come seeking this experience, and of course they find it is not available through the academic process. This obviously is not the purpose of the academic study of religion, but often the young student has serious misconceptions on this point.

By a vital and creative Christian experience, we mean one that gives meaning to the total life and work of pastors, and to their human relationships. Since it is grounded in a personal faith and commitment to God as God is in Christ, it is an experience that gives the person a solid sense of identity before God, and therefore before human beings. It is an experience which leads persons to openness toward themselves and their own motivations rather than to a projection of their anxiety, guilt, or hostility onto others. At this stage most students cannot be expected to have achieved a fully mature love, but they have a sense of their need for growth in this respect. Their experience of forgiveness is still progressing. They have not yet arrived. They are searching for a new understanding of themselves and their relationships with others, and they are conscious of their

124

need to overcome whatever obstacles they may face in deepening their relationships to others. They have the kind of honest appreciation of both their own strengths and their weaknesses that is the basis of humility. They have some awareness of their tendency to manipulate others in order to avoid facing their own problems. Their lives are open to the influence of the Holy Spirit, so that the fruits of the Spirit are gradually becoming realized in them. They have a sense of the genuine freedom of the Christian person, but subject themselves to the fundamental discipline of a love that demands that they seek for others what they seek for themselves. They do not feel under compulsion to accept, and to insist that others accept, a specific formulation of Christian experience, but they are concerned with the reality behind any theological formulation. This statement is far from exhaustive, but it will serve to emphasize that the roots of pastoral care for and to students are in Christian experience.

Our emphasis on communication through relationships is not to be taken to mean that vigorous intellectual training and mastery of intellectual disciplines are not important for the pastor. Emphasis on intellectual training can be detrimental to the pastor when it excludes relational aspects of the ministry as unimportant. On the other hand, many mistakes are made by "well-intentioned" pastors who lack knowledge. Genuine love toward God and human beings includes both knowing them directly and knowing about them. Thus pastors need to be highly intelligent persons who have subjected themselves to the discipline of study. Absence of this background will tend to destroy the trust of others in them. Sound knowledge is one dimension of a helping pastoral relationship with people.

One of the needs of seminaries today is to learn what it means to promote the growth of the whole person rather than merely to give lip service to this idea. Such ideas as "the growth of the whole person" easily catch the imagination, but enthusiasm wanes when specific suggestions are made for implementing them. On the whole, theological education tends to be very conservative and to follow the church rather than furnish leadership. Or it may tend to confine its leadership to the realm of ideas, and discount the world of functional realities.

One of the fundamental questions raised by the pastoral-care movement is: What should be the perspective of theological education in its curriculum-building and its teaching? The standard answer given by most seminaries to this question is scholarship. The seminary is a community of scholars; each member of the faculty is expected to be a scholar in a particular field. Latest findings in biblical, theological, historical, and other aspects of scholarship in religion are brought to the student. European scholarship is highly revered in the seminary, and sometimes idolized. In fact, scholarship often is rated much more highly than the ability to be a good teacher.

But there is a certain dilemma in the scholarship perspective. How is it to be made meaningful and relevant to the pastor and the problems of persons? This dilemma is often reflected in the inability of students to see the relevance of what they are studying for what they hope to do, or are doing, in the pastorate. Part of this failure may be owing to the student's lack of experience, but in part it is because scholarship is relevant to scholarship, but not necessarily to the problems of the pastorate. Some of the problems of biblical and theological scholarship are so far removed from the problems of human existence that no amount of imagination can make them relevant. Quite justifiably scholarly problems have to do with technical issues in a given field, not with what goes on in persons and between persons or between persons and God.

One of the serious effects of the scholarship perspective upon the personality of the theological student is a confused sense of identity. Many students come to seminary with some confusion as to their personal and professional identity. Three or four years of study under "scholars" forces them into a position of either identifying with these teachers and accepting themselves as scholars or rejecting this identity for themselves. For those of high intellectual capacity, such positive identification is not as difficult as it is for those with more limited capacities, and academic rewards are a further encouragement. Students then see themselves as essentially "scholars and teachers" (these activities are closely associated in our culture), rather than as pastors. Students who take a negative stand toward scholarship (and some students of high ability do this because of conflicting personality needs) tend to discount learning for the pastor and work on their hunches, or to give their own personal needs full control of their work. This negative identity — what individuals feel they should not be — is frequently expressed in the seminary graduate who stops studying seriously after leaving seminary. The question we are raising here is this: What basis for identity as a pastor — in the full meaning of this term — does the scholarship perspective offer theological students? Does it lead them away from responsible functioning as pastors?

Let it not be assumed that in raising this question we are against scholarship in the seminary. We are decidedly for it, and at certain points would add to it; but this is not the issue. The issue is: How, in an atmosphere of scholarship, can the student gain a positive basis for identity as a pastor? How, in an atmosphere that emphasizes books, ideas, examinations, grades, intellectual controversies and issues, and the necessary technical aspects of scholarship — how, in the atmosphere of the academy — do we help students get a working and workable image of themselves as pastors? To say that much of the scholarship in the seminary deals with the existential problems of life, with which the pastor also deals, misses the point. For the academic approach of the seminary deals with these issues — sin, salvation, guilt, hate, love, death, suffering, and the like — intellectually, academically, and rationally, and often comes out with formulations that are of no value to a person in the actual throes of suffering. The perspective from which we deal with the issues is the point here. For example, a philosophical or theological course on the problem of suffering may help students to think through some of the intellectual problems related to suffering, to evaluate various interpretations and notions about suffering, and to clear away a lot of hazy thinking on the subject. But when they face a person who is suffering, they will need to be not a philosopher, but pastors such as we have been describing in this book. Intellectual discipline should be one aspect of pastors' training, but by itself it is insufficient for their needs.

How then can the scholarly emphasis of the seminary be utilized to help students develop an identity as pastors, the kind of identity they need if they are to become real pastors and not something else? The answer which we shall give to this problem will hardly be acceptable to most seminary faculties. For the fact is that the very qualities that make a person a good scholar may not be those that make a good pastor, and we all have to use the talents we have been given.

Our suggestion, however, is that seminary teachers should not only be scholars, they should also be pastors. By this is meant that they should have a continuing responsibility as pastors with one congregation — part time, of course — and thus become involved deeply in the life of one congregation. Of course they would have to have assistance, depending on the size of the parish, but in some cases their students could be given a creative learning experience by serving as their assistants. Such relationships would give students a basis for developing an identity as a pastor. They would see their teacher not only as a scholar but as a pastor, a pastor whose scholarship finds expression in pastoral pursuits. The frequent complaint about the irrelevance of so much scholarship would no longer be heard. Such relationships would bring new perspectives on curriculum planning and teaching and give teachers the material through which they could integrate, in reality rather than in the abstract, the area of their scholarship with the actual situation in the parish.

We shall not deal here with objections that will be launched against this idea. Some of these will be real and some fanciful, but they are obstacles to be overcome if theological education is to bring new life into the church. Teachers in the seminary may see themselves as pastors, but students do not see them this way. The seminary today has identified itself with the academy — and the teacher with the academician — rather than with the profession for which it is seeking to train people. This is the situation that needs to be modified. We are not offering a blueprint of how this is to be done, since it will be achieved, if at all, in terms of differing local conditions and denominational polity. It is obvious that our suggestion would bring radical changes in the structure of theological education that could be worked out only with considerable time and experiment.

Not only does the faculty need continual encounter with the life of a parish, but so does the student! Theological education today is grounded on a very serious fallacy, namely, that ideas and values become incorporated into the functioning processes of students through verbal communication. On the contrary, both general observation and scientific studies indicate clearly that for creative learning students must become involved in the processes and structures they are studying.[1] Very frequently theological students have not had experience in the area in which a professor is lecturing. Therefore the professor's ideas sound unreal, or completely irrelevant, or even threatening. Students may learn them by rote and pass their examinations, but be unable to incorporate them into their thinking and acting. Or they may find themselves unable to learn these ideas — without understanding why. Students who fight with unreal or threatening ideas may come out better in the long run if they permit themselves to be motivated by their irritations to continue the struggle with their problem. Ideas, attitudes, and values are learned or changed only in situations where teacher and student are both involved in a third dimension, that is, the reality that is under consideration.

This means that the curriculum and teaching of the seminary must be grounded in the involvement of the teacher and student in the ongoing life of a parish. Laypersons must of necessity become a part of this process, since they are the center of the life of the parish. It is for them that sermons are given, educational programs projected, services of worship held, funerals and weddings conducted. It is their growth and welfare with which we are concerned, their salvation for which we pray, and their understanding of the faith that merits the pastor's attention. The deep crises met in pastoral care are those in the lives of laypersons, whether death or illness or some other kind of emotional and spiritual separation. Laypersons are being told that they should carry the message of the gospel into the community, into business, and into the world. But they must be equipped in mind and spirit to do this.

It is amazing that theological education can proceed with so little concern for the persons with whom pastors are to work: the laity in our church and the persons in our community. Thus it is not surprising to hear ministers complain about the demands and needs of the laity as though these were burdens. To inadequately trained and improperly oriented ministers these demands are burdens, not opportunities. It is not surprising that laypersons think that theological education is missing the point!

Teacher, student, and layperson need to become involved in a living encounter in the task of theological education. Curriculum and teaching should be organized around the experience of the student and teacher in actual parish situations, with actual persons. This calls for a radical departure from the present methods of the seminary. The new approach would go far beyond what is usually called "field work," since it would include all departments. There is a gnawing conviction in the minds of many theological professors today that we are failing to reach our students in any profound way. To overcome this anxiety we add more courses, increase requirements, and do other such things to bolster up a curriculum and methodology that needs radical change. Theological education needs to be centered on the involvement of student, layperson, and teacher with each other and with the Christian faith.

Let it be clear that we are not suggesting more "experience" for theological students in a church. Many students today are getting experience in student charges, but they do not have the foggiest idea as to how to relate their "experience" to their studies in the seminary. Furthermore, their experience is only a vague reality. They do not know how to go about discovering its meaning because they are unable to see what is there. In counseling courses it is usual to have students report on their interviews, which they have recorded verbatim; but they often do not see the meaning of what they have written down. The same lack of meaning is true in other aspects of their parish experience.

This does not intend to be critical of the students. For they are the products of an educational system that has taught them ideational structure, but has not enabled them to understand reality and its functioning. They have been taught to be dependent on their teachers and not to take initiative in thinking, and they have learned this lesson well. They have also been taught that imagination is a wonderful tool, but that it should be used very sparingly since we must deal with facts. Therefore they cannot see relationships between facts, and they cannot understand meanings and values beyond facts. Also, they have been carefully taught to repress their own feelings and emotional conflicts and to exercise various psychological defenses, with the result that they cannot enter empathically into the experiences of other persons and participate in their meanings and sufferings. Theological education tends to reinforce these inadequate teachings.

Students need help to discover what they are experiencing: to face and understand the feelings and reactions this event arouses in them and then to seek to understand what it means to others who are involved, to ask what it means in the light of the Christian faith and what is needed to enable others to enter into creative Christian meanings. Students need help in penetrating beneath the verbalisms of the faith to the very real and creative processes and meanings to which these verbalisms may point. Since such help is essentially the task of the teacher, teachers themselves are required to be involved experientially in all the crucial issues of a parish, and to some extent in the life of the student. The task of teachers is not to pour ideas into the minds of students, but to awaken in them the latent processes that lead to insight and understanding.

Again we are offering no blueprint for such theological education. Here and there it is already being carried out in the work of individual teachers. The full impact of what we are saying may have to wait for a new generation of teachers who have participated in such learning experiences as students. We are not suggesting that the ancient and revered "content" of theological education be ruled out. But by some means there needs to be a creative synthesis of content with real pastoral involvement, in which these dimensions of religious faith are permitted to speak to each other. Such speaking will take place through the mind and heart of the student and teacher in a mutual learning encounter — one in which the student is given the freedom and responsibility to combine a Christian interpretation of life with daring imagination and is helped to cultivate a spirit sensitive to human need. This means the deep involvement of the student, teacher, and layperson around the profound issues of human life and the life of the church, past, present, and in the immediate future. To be sure, the ultimate dimensions of the Christian faith must become both the motivation and the goal of such an educational process, but again these must find expression and be authenticated in living persons rather than in verbal structure. For the Word of God is a Person — a Living Person — or, as Paul says, our faith is futile (1 Cor. 15:17–19).

We have already indicated the need for extending the scholarly pursuits of the seminary. We believe this should be done in the area of what is known today as the behavioral sciences —

psychology, psychiatry, and the dynamics of personality-culture relationships. Again we do not offer a blueprint for carrying this out, since there is more than one way. However, the main concern is that it be done.

This emphasis is not entirely missing in seminary curriculums today. However, considering the function pastors might fulfill in the lives of persons, much more stress needs to be given in this area. Furthermore, pastors should be familiar with, and be able to utilize, some of the methods and approaches of these disciplines. For pastors are in an exceedingly strategic position in the field of human growth. They stand in a crucial position between individual and cultural dynamics and no profession has more opportunity for either good or evil influence than ours. But more than this, pastors can render much of their religious ministry ineffective by not having a basic and workable knowledge of the individual, social, and cultural influences that shape human life in our church and community. Furthermore, pastors need to have an appreciation of the work of the leaders in the behavioral science fields.

This last point is important. One of the intellectual dangers of theological education is that an attempt is made to put knowledge through a critical analysis from a given theological point of view. There is necessity and value in this. But such an analysis must proceed not only from an understanding of theology, but also from within the field that is being evaluated. Otherwise many of the negative criticisms offered will be as absurd as some of the theological criticisms of psychoanalysis have been in the past. They have been made out of anxiety or hostility rather than of understanding. But even more important, the behavioral sciences are here to stay, and they will see great development in the years ahead. The love of truth that the Christian faith commands should teach us to appreciate the positive contribution of these sciences to the work of the church and lead us to use their contribution for the benefit of persons.

There is another aspect of this problem. Those theologies that consider themselves immune to criticism and evaluation from other points of view will eventually lead nowhere. For theological concepts, like concepts in any field, need to expand and grow in meaning, or else they become dead. The behavioral sciences are producing material that should be considered, and to some extent related to the theological concept of the human being. Part of the task of the seminary is to help the student begin this process of synthesis. We say "begin," because this is a lifelong process, not to be confined to the years of seminary experience.

The danger that some will see here is that we turn students away from their central task as pastors and make them into psychologists or "amateur psychiatrists." This is a part of the problem of identity discussed above. Some students come to seminary with a strong sense of pastoral identity — they want to go into the pastorate to help persons. At some point in their earlier Christian experience they have caught this vision. Their training in seminary, however, does not seem to fit them for this task, and when they get into the parish they find many obstacles, one of the chief being their lack of training in fields that help them to understand persons. So somewhere along the line, in seminary or in the early years of their ministry, they shift their vocational plans and enter one of the other helping professions. Or they leave the parish ministry and go into some form of specialized ministry such as hospital chaplaincy or pastoral counseling. The real problem here is not that they have been taught something that is foreign to the ministry. It is that they have not been trained adequately to help persons as pastors, and then they may have found the organizational structure of their church operating against such activities. One answer to this problem is better education in the behavioral sciences, a more effective integration of this education with the theological perspective, and more effective training in the arts and skills of helping persons as pastors. It has been my privilege to enter deeply into the experiences of a number of such students and pastors, and I have never found persons leaving the ministry because their training in the behavioral sciences was too great or their skills in helping others too effective. There is a tragic attrition in the parish ministry, but for other reasons.

Another essential approach in the making of pastors is clinical pastoral training. We will not repeat at length the various testimonials to the value of clinical pastoral training. It is sufficient to point out that such training, when carried out properly, cannot be reproduced in the classroom. Nor is there any other kind of theological training that produces the same values. The major advantage of clinical pastoral training is experience in personal and pastoral relationships under supervision. In the classroom we can *talk* about relationships; but in clinical pastoral training students *experience* relationships in a context in which they are helped to understand what is actually going on between themselves and others. The fact that in this case the others are either persons who are sick in one way or another, or they are fellow students or professional helpers such as doctors and nurses, gives the student and the supervisor the opportunity to explore various kinds of relationships that are experienced by the student. Of course, the central problem is the relationship of patient and pastor. Theological education needs to accept and act upon the fact that the discussion of relationships in the classroom is no substitute for the actual experience of relationships under supervision. And no other branch of theological education has developed the art and practice of supervision in relationships more fully than has clinical pastoral education.

Today there is a movement toward what is being called "clinical pastoral training in the parish." It might be better if the word "clinical" were left off; on the other hand, its use does indicate that the methods developed by the clinical pastoral training movement are being applied in the parish. This is all to the good — just what is needed to transform the seminary "field work" of the past into a meaningful educational experience. There are special problems in such training in the parish that are far from being surmounted today, although there are some encouraging experiments.

One basic problem for the seminary in the clinical pastoral training movement, whether in the institution or in the parish, is the development of supervisors and the relation of the supervisors to the seminary faculty. Among the conditions making for an uneven quality of supervision, in the clinical pastoral training movement as a whole, are: the rapid growth of the movement in the past decade, the process of accrediting supervisors, the refusal or inability of the seminaries to become deeply involved in clinical pastoral training, the fear in some quarters of what they describe as an undue psychiatric emphasis in clinical pastoral training. A close cooperation between the seminary and local centers, with the inclusion of the clinical training supervisor in the regular faculty of the seminary, would make for real advances. As long as clinical pastoral training is kept on the periphery of theological education it will not be able to make its full contribution.

We have already referred to the professional importance of pastors' identity as persons. Pastors need a clear and firm sense of themselves as persons as a basis for entering into the experiences of others in a pastoral relationship.

To elaborate on the problems involved in the struggle for ego identity in American youth is beyond the scope of this chapter. Many theological students suffer from the same kinds of identity conflict as do many other young persons in our culture. This may be due to weaknesses in the culture that prevent it from offering a solid basis for identity. Or it may be due to conflicts in youth that prevent them from accepting the identity the culture provides. It may be grounded in inadequate interpersonal relationships. At least, many youths in our culture grow up without experiencing a deep sense of their value and meaning to themselves and to others. This frequently finds expression in vocational conflict and inability to make vocational decisions. It also finds expression in sexual conflicts, an extreme example of which would be the youth who prefers homosexual contacts. And it also finds expression in youth's approach to religion. Many of the religious problems of this age — problems of belief, of faith, of action — are rooted in the inability of young persons to discover who they are before others and before God. Erikson's description of the identity conflict in Martin Luther, in *Young Man Luther,* has many parallels in theological students today.[2] Bowers, in *Conflicts in the Clergy,* gives a picture of some extreme examples of identity conflicts in ministers, counterparts of which are to be found in any theological seminary.[3]

Theological students bring their problems of identity, mild or severe, with them to the school.[4] And consciously or unconsciously they seek to work them out in the academic experience. This means that their study of theology, Bible, and other seminary disciplines is motivated by deep personal needs of which they may or may not be aware. In attempting to resolve intellectual problems, they are trying also to discover who they are and their relation to knowledge. Thus, wrestling intellectually with the problem of God, or of guilt, or of the meaning of life, or of history, or of being, to mention just a few possibilities, they are also wrestling with something very important within themselves. They are seeking so-called "objective" knowledge as a basis and guide for subjective experiences. And they may be projecting a great many of their own feelings and conflicts onto "objective" knowledge, so that what they believe to be objective is really more the reflection of their own inner world. Or they may find that academic requirements seriously interfere with their personal pursuit of truth as determined by their own needs. Here again they may face the problem of following their own sense of being or of conforming to cultural demands. If they do the former, they may fail in their studies; if they do the latter, they will sacrifice their own integrity and accept dependence on authorities for what no authority can really give them.

The way in which students resolve this problem, both emotionally and intellectually, will have far-reaching effects on their capacity to become pastors. For whatever pastoral relationships they create with others will in part reflect the kind of solution they have found to this problem.

The seminary therefore needs to see its academic functions in the light of the profound need of students to find an intellectual frame of reference in which they can stand and from which they can function in the process of discovering their own identity. This means that the seminary must combine its academic purpose with something of a therapeutic purpose. We are speaking of the emotional and intellectual climate of the classroom, of the teacher-student relationship, of the opportunity of students to pursue some of their own interests and needs, and of teachers who are more concerned with helping students learn *how* to think than with *what* they think. There is no doubt that many seminary students are searching for these values in their intellectual experience. Nor is there any doubt that some teachers are aware of this and are assisting students creatively. But the situation needs a wider recognition and a more conscious provision for its constructive handling throughout the total process of theological education.

If the seminary is truly interested in the "whole person," it has another responsibility that in no way conflicts with its intellectual task. Theological education must become as concerned for the emotional growth of students as for their intellectual growth and make adequate provisions for helping them on this level. A highly trained intellect in an emotionally immature or sick person can be destructive in the ministry. Students with the kind of mild emotional patterns that handicap them in their personal relationships should also be a focus of concern.

There is no one approach to this problem. Essentially students need an experience of self-discovery, that is, an experience of self-understanding and the kind of growth that comes through this process, or at least an opportunity for this experience. Some opportunities may occur in certain kinds of classes, some in worship, some in various small-group experiences. However, a more systematic approach would be through a staff of well-trained pastoral counselors, supplemented by psychotherapists where needed. A question here is the level of personal help to students for which a school should accept responsibility, and the point at which students should be asked to accept the financial responsibility. We are not advocating that seminaries make long psychotherapy available to its students without cost.

One of the needs of theological students in their first year is the opportunity to examine their motives for going into the ministry and the suitability of their kind of persons for the work of pastors. A staff of pastoral counselors should be available for this. For many theological students a relatively short period of counseling would be sufficient for needed insight and growth. Others would require a longer period.

The value of this approach for the teaching program of the seminary needs to be explored. However, it would seem that theological education should begin not only with what great thinkers have said, but also with what the students believe and say. Until students have come to terms with themselves religiously and theologically, they are hardly in a position to really appreciate the contribution of others. Theological study that is not accompanied by sufficient opportunity for personal insight may become a matter of rationalization and projection — the more brilliant the intellect, the more proficient in this. For deep, unconscious reasons, students may find themselves inordinately drawn toward one particular authority or position, while they are repelled by others that really deserve their unbiased consideration. Also, some students must settle emotional conflicts with their parents before they are really in a position to clarify their faith or relationship with God. This is not an intellectual process and is less likely to take place in a classroom than in a counseling process. Religious and theological studies may become so entangled with unconscious hostilities, anxieties, and guilt feelings that students are either driven compulsively or blocked and inhibited, without knowing why. Or, as we have indicated previously, students may succeed in divorcing their intellect from their feelings, and pursue a cold, intellectual, so-called objective approach to religious thought, while their emotional life remains childish or even infantile. Genuine objectivity in matters of vital concern to pastoral care is grounded in a positive faith, a fairly unambivalent commitment, and mature love. It is not devoid of feeling and not coldly objective.

And we should not neglect the value of this approach for the teaching of subjects in the field of pastoral care. So many of the problems in church administration and field-work supervision resolve themselves into problems of personal attitude and relationship. The teaching of preaching, religious education, and counseling is so much more than the teaching of techniques and intellectual content. It is helping students grow emotionally until they become persons who can enter adequately into the teaching or preaching or counseling tasks required of them. Instead of the multiplication of courses and the lengthening of the seminary program, more attention given to the emotional growth of students would contribute greatly to their effectiveness as teachers or preachers, or in any aspect of pastoral care. It would also remove obstacles to learning, and hence decrease certain curricular pressures.

Much of what we have been saying in this chapter may be symbolized by two words, "scholar" and "saint." The symbol that expresses the goals of most theological schools today is the scholar. Strong pressure in this direction is felt from within the schools and from other academic disciplines. But we need to ask just what is this scholarship that pastors need? Could it be that we are trying to project into theological education some kinds and areas of scholarship that are not relevant to the pastoral task even though they may have some connection with religion? And could it be that we need to add to the theological curriculum some areas of scholarship that are now being neglected?

But deeper than this, we need to balance the symbol "scholar" with another symbol, "saint." Saints are persons who are growing in genuine love toward God and others, who are honestly trying to cope with the conditions in themselves that are obstacles to such love, and who are able and willing to use professional services to this end. They take seriously the statement of Jesus about removing the beam from our own eye so we can see clearly to remove the mote from our brother's or sister's eye. They not only "know" in the sense of scholarship, but they know in the sense of the ability to enter directly and deeply into the experiences of others. They may have been persons who were once seriously sick emotionally, but because they have endured the suffering involved in finding wholeness, they can now enter into the suffering of others, whether in groups or in individual relationships. Saints are people who are growing toward the fulfillment in their own person of the words of Paul about the fruits of the Spirit (Gal. 5:22), or his words in the thirteenth chapter of 1 Corinthians. Pastors should not be scholars only. If they are not saints in the meaning we have expressed here, they will not be genuine pastors. In the last analysis we would have to say that becoming a saint is the work of God, but God has given us a responsibility in the process, and we have been talking about some ways to fulfill that responsibility. Many of the major obstacles to creative pastoral relationships have developed in human experience, and they will be cured through human agencies. It is better from the pastoral point of view that these human agencies be also committed to the Christian faith, although we must add, on the basis of our experience, that this is not absolutely essential. The reality of the curative power of genuine love and understanding is essential.

The church, Christian theology, and theological education today are very concerned about the great problems of our culture, the problems of war and peace, of human justice and welfare, of health and illness, of marriage and the family, and of economic conflict, to mention only a few. Every pastor grows up in a culture, and being human we are likely to participate in the illnesses of that culture. The church must necessarily make pronouncements on various social problems so that the world knows where it stands. But it faces a greater challenge. Can it devise a means of theological education of the whole person to help its future pastors become comparatively free of the illnesses of their culture, so that in turn they may become effective Christian pastors to persons in that culture and thus help to cure some of its illnesses? For without discounting the value of social action, in the final analysis the cure of the illnesses of our culture will depend upon helping individual persons to become whole, in the New Testament meaning of that phrase.

NOTES

1. See Kurt Lewin, *Resolving Social Conflicts* (New York: Harper & Row, 1948), chap. 4. Also, Carl Rogers, *Client-Centered Therapy* (Boston: Houghton Mifflin Co., 1951), chap. 9.

2. Erik Erikson, *Young Man Luther* (New York: W. W. Norton, 1958).

3. Margaretta Bowers, *Conflicts in the Clergy* (New York: Thomas Nelson & Sons, 1963).

4. Today certain groups are offering scholarships for students who are not committed to the ministry to study in a theological seminary. Limited experience with such programs suggests that many of these students have identity needs that will never be resolved by a purely academic approach, and that these programs need to add a therapeutic dimension.

<$\prec$ **7** $\succ$>

Culture and Care

by John E. Hinkle, Jr.

Communication occurs in context, a point Wise makes repeatedly. This final chapter takes that point as central to the task of revising the foregoing text. More accurately, the task of updating Wise is more one of "re-contexting" than of revising. The following discussion will focus on some features of the pastoral care situation Wise faced, with suggestions for re-contexting some phases of his thought in selected but crucial aspects of the current context of pastoral care. Further, since context inevitably influences content, some implications of context for content will be noted. Definitions of optimal personhood and changes in gender role definition will be presented as examples of areas in which it is necessary to re-context the meaning of pastoral care. Resources and methodological suggestions will be provided in order to assist readers in doing their own "translation" of this important work into the context in which they function.

The context that generated *The Meaning of Pastoral Care* had particularities of its own, as well as commonalities consistent with the context of pastoral care since that time. The process of translating content from one context to another can provide a means for further clarification of the central and enduring features of the message. The focus of this chapter is selective rather

than comprehensive. Readers are invited to engage in the translation and revision process themselves, as appropriate to their
own context.

The Central Message

After addressing the biblical and theological frame of reference
within which he sets his work, Wise defines pastoral care as the
art of communicating the inner meaning of the gospel to persons at the point of their deepest need. He then unfolds the
various aspects of this definition: Pastoral care is the communication (through relationships that mediate the reality being
communicated) of the inner meaning of the gospel (which is the
personhood of Jesus as interpreted and understood through the
work of the Holy Spirit in the context of loving human relationships) to persons (who are unique, aware, private, and autonomous) at the point (whether proximate or ultimate) of their need
for healing (crisis or conflict resolution and movement toward
wholeness [integration] or psychosomatic health) or growth (development through the human life cycle and movement toward
maturity of spirit).

By defining pastoral care in this way Wise endeavors to speak
to the pastor as person, and as person-in-relationship. The pastor is portrayed as the kind of person who can be interpersonally
present to others in ways that both enable and validate (incarnate) faith. This pastoral presence (as person and as mediator) is
characterized by empathy, mutuality, concern, spontaneity, maturity, and understanding based on the subjective experience of
self and the empathic experience of the other, and in the light
of relevant theory from the personality and social sciences, as
well as theological and faith-related perspectives. Relationships
that result from this model of pastoral presence are characterized as loving and potentially redemptive. Words and concepts
in these relationships flow from the experience and give accurate expression to it. In this process words are experientially
meaning-full, hence meaningful. The purpose of pastoral care
is to provide a loving relationship within which the individual
will be able to experience meaning. This meaning brings together the idiosyncratic and the ideological (i.e., the religious
and cultural formulation of meaning). The goal of pastoral care

is to enable the individual to participate fully and spontaneously in communal and creedal meanings, a participation made possible when the individual's experience and its meaning become functional. The work of the Holy Spirit is seen as intrinsic to this internal-relational process, without that work being limited to this intrapsychic/interpersonal process only. The work of the Holy Spirit in this process may be thought of as enabling persons who are made in the image of God to attain that likeness, that is, to achieve their full potential and to move toward perfection of spirit. The fruits of the Spirit noted by St. Paul (Gal. 5:22) provide some expression of growth in this dimension.

This question will guide the present discussion: Are there elements in the way Wise has formulated the meaning of pastoral care that continue to be useful in the current context of pastoral care? The question may also be stated as follows: Which aspects of Wise's enterprise are bound by time and context, requiring deletion or ongoing revision? Final answers cannot be given to these questions. Suggestions can be made, however, based on a re-analysis of context and the effort to apply the model of pastoral care that Wise presented during his lifetime to present-day constituencies and cultures other than those for whom he wrote.

Wise's Context

Wise was writing in the early 1960s on the basis of problems observed and lessons learned over a twenty-five year span from the 1930s to the late 1950s. He notes in the original publication that the problems he is addressing, "... have been emerging during the past four decades" (p. ix, above). He asserts that the question is "How and under what conditions do the various structures of religion become meaningful to persons?" (p. ix). Wise seeks to answer this question by setting pastoral care within the context of the gospel, rather than within the context of traditional approaches to pastoral care, i.e., administrative, ecclesial, liturgical, and the like. Further, he addresses the issue in terms of the meaning of the gospel and pastoral care in the context of the growth of persons, and in terms of the centrality of relationship to the growth of persons. Finally, he endeavors to "... relate the theological dimension of pastoral care to the personal dimension ... " (p. ix), showing how energy and meaning flow from experience to the symbol rather than from the symbol to experience.

Wise was concerned that pastoral care, when formulated as an activity of the pastoral role, would end up as a manipulation of the parishioner for the pastor's individual and institutional ends, rather than serve individuals "at the point of their needs for healing and growth." Further, he was concerned that pastoral care would continue to involve the indoctrination of individuals with the concepts (theological systems) of church, tradition, and pastor, hence contributing to the suppression of the growth of parishioners as persons (moving them toward conformity and dependence rather than toward creativity and autonomy). These procedures and consequences he saw as operationally and conceptually contrary to the gospel. He therefore emphasized the personhood and relational capacity of the pastor as basic to the communication of the gospel in pastoral contacts.

From the cultural perspective, these problems as stated by Wise continue to be significant and difficult issues in pastoral work and theological training in religious institutions to the present time. For example, a recent nationwide survey of pastoral concerns by a major Protestant denomination revealed that the leading concern experienced by pastors, and one for which they expressed a desire to have continuing education experiences, was the need for better interpersonal relations skills.[1] This finding fits with the conclusion of Trotter, writing in the volume *Ministry in America*, that, " ... a very high valuation [is] placed by the United Methodist respondents on interpersonal leadership and expectations in ministry.... Interpersonal counseling, group dynamics, and the vocabulary of educational psychology dominate the responses of United Methodists."[2] With reference to the problem of telling (indoctrinating) rather than listening, Houts observes, "In teaching groups of lay pastors over the last ten years, I have seen that woeful lack of training, anxiety, and naive zeal are frequently factors which cause many inexperienced pastors to talk too much and to trust their verbal answers far more than experience warrants."[3] Evidence and illustrations that the central problem addressed by Wise continues to the present day could be multiplied. Yet there is little need to do so since cultural change and paradigm shifts have occurred that make awareness of the problem more widespread today than was the case when Wise was teaching and writing. The problem is further exacerbated, however, by these paradigm shifts, a matter that subsequent discussion elaborates.

The problems addressed by Wise within the monocultural context of his era meant preserving the essential spirit of Christian pastoral care modeled on the person of Jesus Christ. This involved relationships of love and concern for others focused on human growth to enable the individual to move from experience to symbols, from dependency and immaturity to autonomy and maturity. Such problems are deepened and become more complex as a consequence of paradigm shifts resulting in new images of optimal personhood, new ways of doing theology, and the need for new ways of encountering the other within the multicultural context of today's world.

The Pentecost Paradigm

The biblical event-experience of Pentecost provides a paradigm for redemptive relationships within a multicultural context. The currently predominant scenario, that is, the culturally encapsulated U.S. Caucasian frame, needs to be informed by the Pentecostal paradigm in which the "breaking out" of the Spirit of Jesus was manifest in a multicultural, multigenerational, and inclusive community of relationships. The suggestion here is that the Incarnational paradigm — with its monocultural dyadic relational model espoused by Wise — be combined with the Pentecostal paradigm — with its multicultural and inclusive community.

The model of pastoral care that Wise proposes is embedded within and flows from a sense of community. Wise does make the point that changed individuals have a major impact on community; such transformed individuals restructure their relationships in more mature and healthier ways. At the same time, the nature of community is largely assumed by Wise and, in the main, serves the function of providing a context within which *individual* change occurs through dynamic pastoral care in dyadic relationships.

Given his concerns, the problems he was seeking to address, the constituency to which he was writing, and the era in which he was addressing those problems, Wise is hardly to be faulted for this feature of his work. Nevertheless, the mindscape and paradigm shifts of the current pastoral care constituency must be taken into account in the application of his Incarnational model of pastoral care. Interestingly enough, while Wise omitted the event-experience of Pentecost in structuring his model of community, he did not neglect the work of the Spirit in his discussions. In fact, the work of the Spirit in intrapsychic and interpersonal processes is elaborated in some detail by Wise. Wise, then, has focused on the work of the Spirit in terms of the central processes of pastoral care, and he has done so in what is for the most part an assumed context.

Wise presents his thinking regarding the work of the Holy Spirit (see pp. 27–34 above) as a pastoral theologian, beginning with what may be experienced in the life of the individual and then moving to biblical and theological materials that further illuminate those motifs. Wise is interested in the experience of the Holy Spirit in intrapsychic and interpersonal terms. He is specifically not interested in notions of the Holy Spirit that are magical or are beyond the ordinary experience of the human person. In the view of some, accounts of Pentecost reflect just such an experience, that is, an event-experience *extraordinaire.*

The biblical account of Pentecost, taken in a literalistic way, describes a historical event of extraordinary proportions. One consequence of that visitation of the Spirit is described as follows:

> Now there were dwelling in Jerusalem Jews, devout men from every nation under heaven. And at this sound the multitude came together, and they were bewildered, because each one heard them speaking in his own language. And they were amazed and wondered, saying, "Are not all these who are speaking Galileans? And how is it that we hear, each of us in his own native language? Parthians and Medes and Elamites and residents of Mesopotamia, Judea and Cappadocia, Pontus and Asia, Phrygia and Pamphylia, Egypt and the parts of Libya belonging to Cyrene, and visitors from Rome, both Jews and proselytes, Cretans and Arabians, we hear them telling in our own tongues the

mighty works of God." And all were amazed and per-
plexed, saying to one another, "What does this mean?"
(Acts 2:5–12, RSV)

Subsequent verses indicate that those present not only heard the
message and experienced it as meaningful, but believed Peter's
interpretation of the event as a revelation of the purpose of God
in Christ. Three thousand were converted and baptized.

Additionally, Peter's quotation of the words of the prophet
Joel is of interest. He says, in part,

...God declares that I will pour out my Spirit upon all
flesh, and your sons and your daughters shall prophesy,
and your young men shall see visions, and your old men
shall dream dreams; yea, and on my menservants and my
maidservants in those days I will pour out my Spirit....
(Acts 2:17–18)

One partial answer to the question, "What does this mean?" is
that the narrative suggests rather clearly both a homogeneous
communal context and a heterogeneous multicultural, inter-
generational, and inclusive context as paradigmatic aspects of
the work of the Holy Spirit in this initial and hence foundational
event. Following the Wise model we may note that the experience came first and the question about what it meant came after.
Peter then stood up to announce to all present the meaning of
this event as interpreted in terms of the purpose of God.

The feature of this event of most interest to the present discussion is the presentation of the multicultural, multigenerational, and inclusive features of the context within which the
arrival of the Holy Spirit occurred and is interpreted. Biblical
scholars may wish to connect the linguistic and cultural aspects
of this phenomenon with the story of the Tower of Babel. And it
should be so connected. But is there not more to the meaning of
this context than a backward look? The remainder of the Book
of Acts is evidence that the gospel was then taken to "the ends
of the earth," to all types and circumstances of persons, in a
wide variety of cultures, by both young and old, to and through
both male and female.

At Pentecost, experiential understanding in the context of

linguistic diversity was noteworthy, as the text clearly indicates: "...each one heard them speaking in his own language. And they were amazed and wondered, saying, 'Are not all these who are speaking Galileans? And how is it that we hear, each of us in his own native language?'" (Acts 2:7–8). Satisfactory explanations of this phenomenon are missing from the scholarly world. Here we encounter mystery as well as meaning. The symbolic message seems clear. In the event-experience of Pentecost, God fixes what was broken at Babel. A common language is provided by which human beings from a diversity of cultures and speaking different languages hear the same gospel. The mechanism through which this communication occurred is shrouded in mystery. Just *what* happened is a matter of speculation. That something dynamic and transformative *did* happen (and lies behind the miracle story) in the early church is not. And the event seems to prefigure a process that in modern times is known as translation, the communication of the gospel from one cultural frame of reference to another through language as well as relationship.

Translation and Conversion

The Christian faith has been translated across many cultures and through centuries of time. In each of the contexts within which it has taken root, the prevailing culture and the faith have stood in dynamic tension. The faith has had an impact on the host culture, and the host culture has had an impact on the faith. This is a complex and highly delicate matter. In a sense, the faith has both transcended and become embedded in culture. Or, more accurately, faith has been experienced by members of diverse cultures through the language and forms of that particular culture. The experience of faith is beyond words, yet must be put into the language (hence conceptual and perceptual system) available to the member of a given culture. This is the incarnational aspect of the gospel as experienced through faith and expressed through cultural forms. Wise quotes Nida as follows:

> This same fundamental principle [Incarnation] has been followed throughout the history of the church, for God has constantly chosen to use not only words but human beings

as well to witness to His grace; not only the message, but the messenger.... (see above p. 34)

Even more to the point, perhaps, is an article in the *Christian Century* entitled "Christian Missions and the Western Guilt Complex."[4] The author, Lamin Sanneh, a Gambian and a Christian convert from Islam, notes that it was the translation of the Bible into the dialect of the people that had the effect, first, of converting the missionary translator to the host culture and, second, of providing a vehicle for the embedding of the gospel in that culture. In order to carry out the process of translation, the missionary had to identify with the people of that culture and come to understand life from their viewpoint. This process required that the *experienced reality* that lay beneath the cultural expressions (words, stories, behavior) be attended to and that the gospel message then be communicated in language grounded in that reality and therefore understandable in the host culture. As Sanneh notes,

> ... missionaries entered the mission field to convert others, yet in the translation process it was they who first made the move to "convert" to a new language, with all its presuppositions and ramifications. Translation destigmatizes culture — it denies that culture is "profane" — and asserts that the sacred message may legitimately be entrusted to the forms of everyday life (in any culture). Translation also relativizes culture by denying that there is only one normative expression of the gospel; it results in a pluralism in which God is the relativizing center. The Christian insight into this phenomenon carries with it a profound ethical notion, for it opens culture up to the demand and need for change. A divinized, absolutized culture precludes the possibility of change.[5]

Herein lies the connection with Pentecost and with the work of Wise. At Pentecost a culturally diverse group of listeners heard the message of the Galileans. The listeners heard each in his or her own native language, not in the language of the Galileans. That is, for the message to have meaning it would have to be put into the cultural and linguistic frame of reference of the hearer.

In a real sense, we may say that Wise was endeavoring to "translate" (in Sanneh's sense) the gospel realities in language that was more nearly faithful to the needs of persons in the dominant culture as he experienced it (English-speaking, mainline Protestant Caucasians for the most part) and with the original intent of the gospel as he understood it. In this sense, then, Wise intended to work with the dynamic realities of the experience of faith (and unfaith) that both transcend and undergird classical creedal and theological formulation. In pastoral care, he sought to allow faith to speak for itself through the experience of the person in terms that are *meaningful to the person*. Once the experience is available to the individual, as mediated through relationship, then words (cultural symbols) can be used by the individual to express the meaning of that experience. Experience is basic to meaning and prior to the expression of meaning. It would seem possible, then, to transmit Wise's methodology from culture to culture through persons in relationship in a multicultural frame of reference and in any given particular language. Language, as well as relationship, structures meaning.

The linguistic frame of reference within which Wise worked and wrote was comprised of English, Bible, Theology, and Personality Psychology. The dialects he used were North American English, Pauline and Johannine sections of an English translation of the Bible, Pastoral Theology, and Neo-Freudian or "dynamic" Personality Psychology. Hermeneutical principles within this context may be characterized as dyadic: intrapsychic/interpersonal, developmental/dynamic, autonomous/mutual, individualistic/communal, experiential/expressive, spontaneous/coerced, spiritual/psychological, pastoral/theological, private/communicative. Within this linguistic frame, genuineness and authenticity of personhood in relationship are the highest goals; achieving them involves the resolution of intrapsychic and interpersonal conflict in a spirit of openness and compassion. Accompanying this is the recognition that a drive to attain the image of God motivates us, and that strong countervailing forces are at work within us to thwart our efforts to attain that goal, both individually and communally.

These linguistic formulations reflect a particular cultural ethos in which interpersonal and personal values are a priority. Whether similar values in the same priority would provide redemptive pastoral care relationships in another ethos or culture seems an open question. Another issue is whether one can address both culturally embedded and universally human (or multicultural) issues at one and the same time.

Wise was aware of the significance of the cultural perspective. He notes that, "Much of the work of the pastor falls in this area of the relationship between personality and culture" (see p. 111 above). Also, "The [clergyperson] has a unique contribution to make to the problems of personality and of culture."[6] While there is little doubt that Wise was making these comments from within the monocultural frame of reference of his own work, an awareness of the multicultural frame nevertheless seems to have been present to his thinking. This awareness is evidenced in such statements as, "The future of personality theory lies with the discipline of culture and personality studies."[7] I have addressed the question of whether Wise was working in a monocultural or multicultural frame in detail elsewhere.[8]

Among the paradigm shifts that have occurred over the past two decades that affect the constituency addressed by Wise, the following appear to be of consequence to pastoral care as Wise defines it.

Images of Personhood

Views of optimal personhood vary from culture to culture. Ideal traits appropriate to those views of optimal personhood are prioritized in different ways from culture to culture. For example, views of optimal personhood in traditional Japanese males give precedence to traits that emphasize living in harmony with others:

> A man becomes secure through tightly knit communal activities. In return, he must always adjust himself to group demands and accept the group consensus.... Within his group he is secure, but his security is maintained at the expense of his individual autonomy.[9]

In the Philippines, optimal views of personhood place high value on characteristics that emphasize behaving in ways that preserve "face" and in so doing prevent experiences of shame or shaming.[10] Geertz has identified views of personhood in Bali, Morocco, and Java that he characterizes as dramaturgical, contextual, and quietistic. In describing the Western conception of the person Geertz writes:

> The Western conception of the person as a bounded, unique, more or less integrated motivational and cognitive universe, a dynamic center of awareness, emotion, judgment, and action organized into a distinctive whole and set contrastively both against other such wholes and against a social and natural background is, however incorrigible it may seem to us, a rather peculiar idea within the context of the world's cultures.[11]

Hsu describes this view of the self with the single term "self reliance."[12] The view of optimal personhood adopted by Wise places a high priority on the traits of autonomy, privacy, awareness, and uniqueness, and reflects the "self-reliant" model of optimal personhood described by Hsu.

This view of optimal personhood, while it is of enormous descriptive and operational significance within the perspective of the dominant Western culture, is only one among many such views of optimal personhood found in the world's cultures. The diversity of these ways of conceiving and defining the self becomes particularly important when one seeks to structure pastoral care in a way that enhances self-development, as did Wise.

If pastoral care is to be directed toward self-development, as Wise maintained, then questions arise: What kind of self is to be developed in a given culture? What are the implications of the gospel for such diverse definitions of the self? and What are the implications of a culturally defined self for the gospel? Or, at a more basic level: Is such a conceptualization of the goal of pastoral care relevant to needs as perceived and experienced in that culture? Is the role of pastor defined in that culture in such a way that the term "pastoral care" has meaning? And if so, what meaning does it have? Wise was writing to the ethos of his time to provide answers to the latter questions.

The foregoing analysis suggests that while the basic processes with which Wise was working may be transcultural, the content of that process would clearly need to vary in significant ways from culture to culture, depending in part on the culture's definition of optimal personhood.[13]

Worldview

Shifts in the scientific paradigm are described by Kuhn.[14] Barbour describes both religious and scientific paradigm shifts, and relates these to each other. He notes that "theological doctrines ... seem divorced from human experience. Religious ideas without an experiential basis appear abstract and irrelevant." And later, Barbour states,

> Both the cognitive claims of religion and its living practice must be grounded in experience. If inherited religious symbols are for many people today almost totally detached from human experience, a return to the experiential basis of religion is important for its renewed vitality in practice, as well as for a sound epistemology in theory.[15]

This cultural critique is identical to the critique Wise makes of the problematic use of theological formulations in his day. Wise returns to basic human experience for the understanding and interpretation of religious ideas, as Barbour subsequently suggests. In doing so Wise utilizes a "psychological model" in addition to the "two natures model" of Christology. Barbour discusses Christological models following notions presented by John McIntyre.[16] But Barbour sees these models as in tension and as mutually corrective, rather than mutually exclusive, as does McIntyre. Wise would agree, noting also that the two natures theological model must also be held in tension with the psychological model. Wise is a part of the paradigm shift described by Barbour.

Slater addresses the dynamics of religion in the context of shifts in worldview. He prefers the terms "central symbols" and "interpretive symbols" rather than the language of paradigm and model for his discussion. In Slater's view a central symbol, such as Jesus Christ, is interpreted in terms of secondary symbols: suffering servant, saviour, friend, and so on.[17] By reviewing the utilization of these interpretive secondary symbols, as they signify changes in perception and new understanding of commitment, religious aspects of paradigm shifts in the self-understanding of individuals and groups come into view.

Berger writes about the construction and sanction of religious worldviews from the perspective of the sociology of religion.[18]

> ... Religion has played a strategic part in the human enterprise of world-building. Religion is the human enterprise by which a sacred cosmos is established. Religion legitimates social institutions by bestowing upon them an ultimately valid ontological status, that is, by locating them within a sacred and cosmic frame of reference. This religious legitimation serves to maintain reality — reality as defined in a particular human collectivity.[19]

Berger goes on to discuss secularization as a process that occurs when the religiously sanctioned worldview is no longer credible, in short, when a paradigm shift is underway.

Larsen is able to point out the process through which cultures move in these paradigm shifts. He does this by discussing a mythic (religious) apprehension of reality.[20] Larsen's conception of what we here refer to as paradigm shifts is focused on the "core of meaning" captured in mythic symbols. He identifies four stages in the process of mythic engagement; each of the four may be taken to represent a phase of paradigm shift: (1) mythic identity, when attention is focused within, (2) mythic orthodoxy, when inner and outer reality are related through stable forms, (3) objective phase (or mythic skepticism), when attention is focused without, and (4) suspended engagement, when there is a detachment from both inner and outer symbols for ultimate breakthrough to the transpersonal self.[21] Each of these phases reflects an experience of changing cultural paradigms at the level of worldview and recognizes the function of religious experience as intrinsic to such changes.

Wise was writing during a period of mythic orthodoxy (Stage 2) in the church and a rising mythic skepticism (Stage 3) in the scientific community. He agreed with neither, seeking to enable persons to live in the context of Stage 4, in which the aim is to experience the personal and the transpersonal self in relation to others and in relation to God.

Participants in modern mainstream North American culture have moved more fully into Stage 4, suspended engagement. And in this context Wise's understandings continue to be relevant to the deep needs and yearnings of persons.

Academic, Clinical, and Personality Disciplines

Turning from the mythic to the academic and clinical, an example of paradigm shift is presented by the thinking of Edmund Sullivan. He makes a case for viewing the discipline of psychology as a hermeneutical enterprise. He characterizes the "critical psychology" that he presents as an emancipatory psychology. By this he means, "... it is a psychology with an expressed interest in the possibilities of human freedom and emancipation."[22] Clinebell pursues this idea of freedom and emancipation in terms of pastoral care. He writes, "The overarching goal of all pastoral care and counseling (and of all ministry) is to liberate, empower, and nurture wholeness centered in Spirit."[23] The model of pastoral care presented by Wise provides both theory and method for such liberation, empowerment, and nurture of wholeness centered in Spirit and focused on the human person. Clinebell goes further, indicating that, "Pastoral care must liberate itself from its dominant middle-class, white, male orientation and become more inclusive in its understanding, concern, and methods. It must become transcultural in its perspective, open to learning new ways of caring from and for the poor and powerless, ethnic minorities, women, and those in non-Western cultures."[24] It seems clear, from the point of view articulated by Clinebell, that the task calls for readers' active participation as they "translate" the work of Wise into their current situation in terms of liberation and empowerment.

The self psychology of Heintz Kohut has proposed significant revisions in psychoanalytic understanding of the self in personality and developmental psychology and in therapeutic encounter.[25] In a more radical vein, Donald Spence has called the entire metaphorical structure of psychoanalytic thinking into question on epistemological grounds.[26] On the other hand, Ernest Becker presents a credible effort to relate the development of the individual self to evolutionary, psychological, sociological, cultural, and religious frames.[27] These authors suggest that one impact of the paradigm shift in the philosophy of science, and in the personality sciences, is a re-evaluation of basic, or root, metaphors. One area in which root metaphors are of particular significance to pastoral care and counseling is in the cultural conception of the self, or "optimal personhood" culturally conceived.

A root metaphor for the self is *persona*, the name for the masks actors wore in Greek drama. The metaphorical basis of the self is discussed at length in Brewster Smith's chapter by that name in *Culture and Self*.[28] Wise's understandings of the self are consistent with the views of Kohut. But neither Wise nor Kohut seems to understand that other views of the self are as valid for other cultural contexts as is the one they assume for this culture. For Wise and Kohut, at least by implication, liberation for the self means the movement of self-understanding in the direction of the North American mainstream cultural view of the ideal self. In contrast, the multicultural perspective allows for liberation in self-understanding that may include movement away from the ideal conceptions of the self implicit and explicit in both Wise and Kohut, towards views of the ideal self as proposed by other cultures.

Gender Role Differences

Feminist critiques of developmental and personality psychology as biased by the chauvinistic/paternalistic patterns of past thinking constitute another paradigm shift that affects personality psychology. Details are elaborated elsewhere. The reader is referred to the works of Gilligan, Miller, Schaef, and Ulanov for technical background.[29] Gilligan's major thesis is based in large part on psychoanalytic perspectives and, in particular, on the work of Nancy Chodorow. Chodorow attributes the continuing differences between the sexes to the fact that women are largely responsible for early child care and to the influence of female socialization. Chodorow says, "In any given society feminine personality comes to define itself in relation [to] and in connection with others more than masculine personality does."[30] In psychoanalytic terms this means that women are not socialized to become as individuated as men and have more flexible ego boundaries. Female identity formation is thus more contextual than oppositional in the ongoing relationship with the mother. Gilligan pursues the point by noting that both mothers and daughters remain part of the dyadic mother-child relationship since daughters are experienced as more alike and continuous with mothers. The girl continues to experience herself as involved in issues of merging and separation and in an attachment characterized by primary identification and the fusion of identification and object choice.[31]

In contrast, since mothers experience sons as opposites, they are more likely to push sons out of the preoedipal relationship and sons will be more inclined to curtail their connectedness with their mothers. Male development at an early age is seen as focused on individuation and the defensive firming of ego boundaries. Chodorow rejects the masculine bias of psychoanalytic theory. She asserts that the existence of sex differences in the early experiences of individuation and relationships, the earliest construction of object relatedness, the earliest definition of the self, the earliest threats to individuation, and the earliest creation of defenses create a *different reality* for males and females due to differences in the early mother-child relationships. Girls emerge from this period with a basis for empathy that is central to their self-definition.[32]

From this basic premise, Chodorow has redefined female psychology:

> Girls emerge with a stronger basis for experiencing another's needs and feelings as one's own (or of thinking that one is so experiencing another's needs and feelings). Furthermore, girls do not define themselves in terms of the denial of preoedipal relational modes to the same extent as do boys. Therefore, regression to these modes tends not to feel as much a basic threat to their ego. From very early, then, because they are parented by a person of the same gender...girls come to experience themselves as less differentiated than boys, as more continuous with and related to the external object-world, as differently oriented to the inner object world as well.[33]

Scanlon comments that "in this analysis masculinity is defined through separation and femininity is defined through attachment. Male gender identity will be threatened by intimacy while female gender identity will be threatened by individuation." She then critiques the Erikson model utilized by Wise:

> Erikson suggests in his developmental schema that the sequence for women is different. Intimacy precedes identity as the female comes to know herself as she is known through her relationships with others. Although Erikson posited a difference between male and female development, the male model remained normative in his thought. The Erikson life cycle model is a model of separation (individuation). There are no stages except the first stage of trust vs. mistrust which would prepare the developing person for the attainment of intimacy, the first adult stage. The model is built on successive levels of separateness with attachment viewed as a developmental deficiency.[34]

This difference becomes problematic when the dominant culture defines maturity as increased autonomy, individuation, and independence. Scanlon notes, "The embedded quality of female thought, relationships and social interaction becomes a developmental liability. Woman's failure to individuate (as defined by the masculine model) becomes a failure to develop."[35]

A new paradigm for developmental understandings of the psychology of women suggests the necessity of significant revisions in the normative model of maturity as elaborated by Wise, with particular reference to individuation, hence autonomy.[36] At the same time that revision of Wise's idea of optimal personhood seems in order, themes of mutuality, empathy, and heteronomy are pervasive in the Wise model and can provide a basis for such revisioning.

From Monocultural to Multicultural Perspectives

The necessity for movement from monocultural to multicultural perspectives — as evidenced at Pentecost — is addressed in helpful ways by Dunne, Augsburger, Geertz, and Bohannon, among others.[37] Augsburger speaks decisively to monocultural encapsulation when he writes:

One who knows but one culture knows no culture.... In coming to know a second or third culture, one discovers how much that was taken to be reality is actually an interpretation of realities that are seen in part and known in part; one begins to understand that many things assumed to be universal are local, thought to be absolute are relative, seen as simple are complex; one finds that culture shapes what we perceive, how we perceive it, and which perceptions will be retained and utilized; one realizes that culture defines both what is valued and which values will be central and which less influential.[38]

Dunne describes a process for "passing over into the feelings and perspective of persons," whether from one's own or another culture, and then coming back to one's own self with fresh insight.[39] Bohannon speaks to the limitations that are involved, noting that one can identify with the members of another culture, but can never become fully a member of a culture other than one's own without violation of personal integrity and the loss of the sense of self. She writes:

The greater the extent to which one has lived and participated in a genuinely foreign culture and understood it, the greater the extent to which one realizes that one could not, without violence to one's personal integrity, be of it. This importance of fidelity to one's own culture and one's own standards is mutual. That is what tolerance means: allowing each person their own integrity.[40]

Augsburger points out that, "Disidentification of the self from old cultural identifications leads to rediscovery of the self in at least three contexts — one's own culture, a second culture, and in that unique third culture that always forms on the boundary between the two." "The intercultural person is not culture-free. Rather the person is culturally aware. Awareness of one's own culture can free one to disconnect identity from cultural externals and to live on the boundary, crossing over and coming back with increasing freedom."[41] In this way, a dual cultural identity may be established over time. The individual can move from cultural encapsulation to an intercultural understanding.

The image of crossing over, coming back, and then living in terms of the "third culture that always forms on the boundary between the two" is, in some ways, a rather apt description of the task of the pastor in mediating between two cultures, the biblical culture(s) and the culture of the pastor's own constituency.[42] Further, occupying a "third culture" position is a regular experience of persons who are simultaneously enculturated in two original cultures, each having its own ethos. This is the case with many ethnic minorities who have a place in a larger dominant culture, as it is to a lesser degree for Caucasian females. Blacks and women in the dominant North American culture often have this "third culture" sense of their experience. It is the "intercultural" aspect of this experience that is of interest here.

I have argued elsewhere that both the theory and the method of Wise point toward an intercultural process:

> In addition to the openness of his theory to the meta-cultural and transcultural aspects of human experience, Carroll's methodology reveals the same openness to cross-cultural varieties of human experience. He sought to encounter the culturally other as dialogical partner rather than as detached observer, through and in the cultural frame.[43]

Wise sought to enable others to be themselves as cultural persons, with identity in their own culture of origin:

> Penetration of personal and *cultural* issues and images to the point of achieving transparency about, as well as both emotional and cognitive apprehension of, the point of their interface with the Ultimate in a manner which transforms, is for Wise the primary, dominant, ever-present, and overriding concern of pastoral care and counseling relationships.[44]

Yet as a monocultural model indigenous to the dominant Caucasian culture of his day, the Wise model needs to be taken further. Augsburger is helpful here. He notes that the intercultural pastoral counselor (pastoral care-giver) must move beyond empathy, to "interpathy":

> Interpathy is an intentional cognitive envisioning and affective experiencing of another's thoughts and feelings, even though the thoughts and feelings arise from another process of knowing, and the feelings spring from another basis of assumptions. In interpathic caring, the process of "feeling with" and "thinking with" another requires that one enter the other's world of assumptions, beliefs, and values and temporarily take them as one's own. In interpathic caring, I, the culturally different, seek to learn and fully entertain within my consciousness a foreign belief. I take a foreign perspective, base my thought on a foreign assumption, and allow myself to feel the resultant feelings and their cognitive and emotive consequences in my personality as I inhabit, insofar as I am capable of inhabiting, a foreign context.[45]

In the interpathic approach, relationship and communication are preserved, but the process of taking into account other views of personhood and other views of the world is added. Pentecost is added to Incarnation. Movement from one worldview and language system to another occurs. In such a process, pastoral care can become intercultural, mutual, and liberating rather than imperialistic and oppressive. Pastoral care based on an integration of Wise and Augsburger provides direction and substance to intercultural pastoral care contexts.

Pastoral Theology and Pastoral Care

Another arena in which a major shift may be observed is in the changing metaphors and models currently in use in pastoral theology and pastoral care, changes reflected in the writings of Ashbrook, Gerkin, Browning, Justes, Wimberly, and Capps, among others.[46] The seminal writings of James B. Ashbrook have implications for pastoral care that are yet to be explored. His work on brain functioning and belief systems awaits assimilation into the pastoral care literature. Ashbrook holds that the human mind provides a useful analytic metaphor for understanding the mind of God. The brain has implications for belief. He writes,

> My exploration has carried us toward New Reality, a shift in paradigm, and so brings us back from the Holy City at the end of history to Pentecost in the midst of history. In the paradigm of Pentecost I find pluralism and relativism, the universal and the particular — every people, from every place, with every tongue.[47]

Gerkin and Capps utilize hermeneutics as a metaphor in developing a method for revisioning pastoral care.[48] Browning and Wimberly maintain an avid interest in the moral guidance functions of pastoral care, each in somewhat different contexts. Wimberly is writing to and for the Black community in particular. And Capps has provided a most helpful extension of the work of Erikson in relationship to the moral dimension of pastoral care.[49] Each is writing from the perspective of a perceived pluralism in values and morals and the consequent confusion concerning the nature of the good: the good person, the good society, the good pastor. Browning describes this situation as a loss of a consensual moral context. According to Browning, the once taken for granted consensual moral context no longer can be taken for granted. Along with other writers in the field of pastoral care, he asserts that fragmentation of values and moral strictures on behavior thus create a new context and an altered task for pastoral care ministry.

Wise would not agree with much that Browning writes in developing his approach to understanding pastoral care. Wise would, however, be interested in the connections Capps is able to make between the later work of Erikson and the dynamics of morality. Capps does this by exploring Erikson's list of human virtues and showing how the opposite of each of those virtues is a vice that the Christian church has named. In so doing, Capps has laid a foundation for linking developmental and dynamic views of personality with the broader moral concerns of fitness for human community, at least as that fitness is viewed by the Christian community.

Capps approaches this task from the perspective of Erikson's life cycle model. Capps puts the problem in terms of arrested moral development and the need of persons to become better oriented in their world.[50] Utilizing the Erikson model, he goes much further than Wise. Some of these developments in the thought of Capps are based on elaborations of Erikson's work that were not available at the time Wise wrote. By combining the list of virtues from Erikson's work with a list of vices that are seen as thwarting moral development, Capps is able to include in his analysis the dynamics of the moral life as well as the development of identity. His treatment of shame in the context of relationship to God and the development of Christian identity is rich with insight concerning spirituality and the often difficult movement from vices to virtues in human life.

In juxtaposing the virtues that accompany stages of development with vices that block the positive resolution of ego crises, a link between morality and ego development is made. The interface between morality and the difficulties of pluralism is addressed in terms of the moral guidance function of the pastor under the heading "The Pastor as Moral Counselor."[51] Hence, Capps takes a further step in the direction of including multicultural concerns in his thinking about pastoral care, if largely in terms of their negative impact in contributing to the pluralism of values that contributes to disorientation. However, as Paul Hessert notes, it is precisely in this disorientation that an opportunity for faith occurs.

Capps agrees that disorientation can provide an opportunity for faith to occur. But he does so in an unsatisfactory manner. He does not see this breakdown of cultural assumptions as the paradigm for God's activity. For Capps, such events are an illustration of the eschatological thrust of the teachings of Jesus that occur "at times." Capps concludes his discussion with the image of Jesus as Wisdom Teacher. Here he lifts up the notion of the eschatological thrust of Jesus' teachings as consistent with the Wisdom literature. And he points out, "This eschatological thrust also means that there are times when our efforts to help persons become better oriented in the world clash with God's incursions in the world."[52] The discussion of this point is crucial in our return to the lasting significance of the work of Wise. For it is this seemingly minor point, added almost as an afterthought at the very conclusion of the discussion by Capps, that needs to be placed center stage in pastoral care, in contrast with views of pastoral care that seek to structure the world and the life of individuals within that structured world.

The Occasion for Faith

Hessert suggests that it is *at just these times*, i.e., when the ordinary assumptions of life break down, that we are at the point of being able to have faith in God *rather than* in the structures of cultural belief systems. He writes, "At times, however, an awareness not subservient to the cultural order breaks into life — awareness of limits to cultural 'reality,' questions about its adequacy and validity, doubts about the truth of utilitarian religion and its God."[53] Utilitarian religion then rushes in with cultural answers, however baptized or secular they are. Moral guidance is given. Rational order is restored. There is no more need for faith in God. Rather, one can return to faith in the culture's utilitarian brand of religion.

In contrast with what utilitarian Christian religion teaches and, one may even say, with what moral guidance in particular would teach, Hessert continues,

> the context within which the Gospel is heard is the void opened by loss. It is not the assured possessors who hear but the poor. All loss, from disappointment to death itself, is caught up in *Christ crucified:* the Messiah is dead!... What lies beyond crucifixion as resurrection is not within the safety and certainty of the cultural structure or within the divine support of utilitarian religion....Cultures cannot comprehend — that is, take within their boundaries — resurrection. Resurrection does not rest on the resources of the culture but on the power of the God who is not the deity of utilitarian religion. To help people hear this Gospel and act in its reality is the core of the pastoral role.[54]

Hessert turns to Blake's contrast between innocence and experience for definitional imagery. Innocence is faith in the utilitarian religion of the culture, or, alternatively, cultural naivete and cultural encapsulation. Experience is

...the awareness that life extends beyond its cultural definition precisely where that definition makes reference to infinity and eternity. Experience is awareness of life outside the province of reassurance and legitimation provided by the culture, outside the security of an order on which "practically everyone" agrees, especially the "authorities" and the "experts."[55]

In this context, faith is not a category of culture:

Faith is not the rehearsed beliefs of the culture, not the doctrinal form of utilitarian religion. Faith is to accept life as more uncertain than our worst fears imagine it and more beautiful than our most intense longing can suggest and both at just that point where our accepted consolations and legitimizations show themselves bankrupt. To experience faith is to ground life in the God beyond cultural credos....Pastoral care-givers confused about their role may accept their social definition as agents of the culture responsible for restoring or maintaining its structure. Thus, pastoral care comes to mean individualizing cultural resources for particular cases. It entails restoring the individual's capacity to cope — that is, to live and act within the cultural structure. Many pastors, teachers, and laity understand this to be their primary religious concern.[56]

Writers in the field of pastoral care for the most part seem to join in a definition of pastoral care that seeks to support utilitarian Christian religion in just these ways, in particular those who support the notion of moral guidance as the central function of pastoral care for our time. Others understand that the pastoral care-giver stands at that interface of meanings where experience and symbols come together through insight (faith), and where the meanings of the "third" culture can be born. In the experience of loss, when the ordinary (utilitarian) assumptions of life break down, the possibility of faith beyond utilitarian religion arises. At this interface, the pastoral care person engages in a process of passing over into the subjective life world of the other (if invited and able), with its loss and its potential. As Dunne

puts it, "...seeing the whole world anew as that person sees it."
Dunne continues,

> The technique of passing over is based on the process of
> eliciting images from one's feelings, attaining insight into
> the images, and turning insight into a guide of life. What
> one does in passing over is to try to enter sympathetically
> into the feelings of another person, become receptive to the
> images which give expression to the feelings, attain insight
> into those images, and then come back enriched by this
> insight to an understanding of one's own life which can
> guide one into the future.[57]

Dunne continues the discussion by saying that "the sympathetic
understanding into which one must enter in order to pass over
into the life of another is itself compassion, for it involves a
sharing of feelings and images as well as gaining insight into the
images and feelings."[58]

The Pastoral Care-giver as Translator

This image of the pastoral care-giver has important similarities
to that of the missionary-translator presented earlier. According
to Sanneh, the missionary who came to convert (provide proclamation and moral guidance in a foreign culture) was, through
the process of translation, the one first converted (changed, enlightened, renewed). The task of translation necessitated the
learning of a new culture and called into question the tenets
of the first culture, hence giving rise to the possibility of faith.
This loss of innocence, that is, the questioning of the monocultural view of Christian faith, provided the possibility for insight,
conversion, faith. In this kind of multicultural context, where
monocultural assumptions are broken, Pentecostal power can
be released anew. Life can be seen and understood from alternative points of view. The idolatry of absolutism is destroyed.
Not only the receiver of pastoral care is renewed, but the pastoral care-giver as well. The new reality is apprehended. But
this is not an easy process. The discussion of shame set forth by
Capps is relevant here. The willingness to be exposed, surprised,
revealed, must be present.

Wise calls the difficult movement from experience to faith "insight":

> Insight stands over against the resources of utilitarian religion. It is not an intellectual formulation of a new worldview (insight is not to be confused with explanation), but a unique integration of feeling with understanding. To reach insight is to have passed beyond the need to cover and disguise life in order to put up with it. In this struggle for insight, and not merely helping people deal with their problems, pastoral counseling (care) is no mere adjunct to the parish enterprise but its focus.[59]

The pastoral care-giver reaches out to those who have suffered loss, at the point of their need, seeks to enter into that experience of loss in order to achieve understanding, listens to the translation of that experience of loss into words of suffering and grief (the story), and participates in the hearing-telling of a new story at the interface. Incarnation, Crucifixion, Resurrection, and Pentecost are manifest here.

Wise, as extended by Capps, and further broadened by a multicultural perspective (Augsburger), provides a basis for releasing the pastoral care-giver from imprisonment in monocultural assumptions and the cul-de-sac (idolatry) of monocultural encapsulation. Following Pentecost, the gospel was preached and heard throughout the known world. Communicating the gospel through relationships in ways that enable the meaningful hearing of that gospel remains the central task of pastoral care for our time.

NOTES

1. Richard Yeager, "Continuing Education Needs Survey," Division of Ordained Ministry, Board of Higher Education and Ministry, United Methodist Church, Nashville, Tennessee, 1987, unpublished.

2. F. Thomas Trotter, "United Methodist Church," in *Ministry in America*, ed. David S. Schuller, Merton P. Strommen, and Milo L. Brekke (San Francisco: Harper & Row, 1980), pp. 446, 449. While it may be objected that the United Methodists are only one denomination among many, "... it is a 'national'

church, developed principally in the westward movement of the American frontier, with congregations in most counties of the U.S.A." (ibid., p. 446).

3. Donald C. Houts, "Parish Pastoral Practice: Undermining or Underlining?" in *At the Point of Need: Living Human Experience*, ed. James B. Ashbrook and John E. Hinkle, Jr. (Lanham, Md.: University Press of America, 1988), p. 95.

4. Lamin Sanneh, "Christian Missions and the Western Guilt Complex," *Christian Century*, April 8, 1987, pp. 330–334.

5. Ibid., p. 332.

6. Carroll A. Wise, *Religion in Illness and Health* (New York: Harper & Row, 1942), p. 257.

7. Cited in John E. Hinkle, Jr., "The Living Human Experience across Cultures," in *At the Point of Need: Living Human Experience*, p. 185.

8. Ibid., chap. 16.

9. Chie Nakane, *Japanese Society* (Tokyo: Charles E. Tuttle Co., Publishers, 1973), p. 126.

10. Benoni Reyes Silva-Netto, "Culture, Personality, and Mental Health: An Ethnographic Study of Filipino Immigrant Families," unpublished dissertation, Northwestern University, p. 137.

11. Clifford Geertz, "From the Native's Point of View," in *Symbolic Anthropology: A Reader in the Study of Symbols and Meanings*, ed. Janet L. Dolgin, David S. Kemnitzer, and David M. Schneider (New York: Columbia University Press, 1977), pp. 483–491.

12. Francis L. K. Hsu, "American Core Character," in *Psychological Anthropology: Approaches to Culture and Personality*, ed. F. L. K. Hsu (Homewood, Ill.: Dorsey Press, 1961), pp. 216–220.

13. The argument can be made that as societies become more highly differentiated in terms of social institutions and their derivative roles, the need for the individual to develop autonomy will increase. However, such an argument is typically based on the assumption that institutions the world over are like those of Western civilization and hence require autonomous functioning. Arguments based on such assumptions appear to be in error since social institutions and role requirements are quite diverse in different cultures. See Paul J. Bohannon, *Social Anthropology* (New York: Holt, Rinehart and Winston, 1963), pp. 26–31, 146, 148, 154ff.; Francis L. K. Hsu, *Clan, Caste and Club: A Comparative Study of Chinese, Hindu and American Ways of Life* (Princeton: Van Nostrand and Co., 1961); G. P. Murdock, *Social Structure* (New York: Macmillan, 1949).

14. Thomas S. Kuhn, *The Structure of Scientific Revolutions* (Chicago: University of Chicago Press, 1962).

15. Ian G. Barbour, *Myths, Models and Paradigms: A Comparative Study in Science and Religion* (New York: Harper & Row, 1974), pp. 1, 8.

16. Ibid., p. 153. See John McIntyre, *The Shape of Christology* (London: SCM Press, and Philadelphia: Westminster Press, 1966).

17. Peter Slater, *The Dynamics of Religion* (New York: Harper & Row), p. 91.

18. Peter Berger, *The Sacred Canopy* (New York: Anchor Books, Doubleday Co., 1969), chaps. 1–2.

19. Ibid., p. 35.

20. Steven Larsen, *The Shaman's Doorway* (New York: Harper Colophon Books, Harper & Row, Publishers, 1976), chap. 1.

21. Ibid., p. 42.

22. Edmund Sullivan, *A Critical Psychology: Interpretation of the Personal World* (New York: Plenum Press, 1984), p. 125.

23. Howard J. Clinebell, *Basic Types of Pastoral Care and Counseling* (Nashville: Abingdon Press, 1984), p. 26.

24. Ibid., p. 25.

25. Heintz Kohut, *Analysis of the Self* (New York: International Universities Press, 1971).

26. Donald P. Spence, *The Freudian Metaphor: Toward Paradigm Change in Psychoanalysis* (New York: W.W. Norton, 1987), p. 212.

27. Ernest Becker, *The Birth and Death of Meaning* (New York: The Free Press, 1971).

28. Brewster M. Smith, "The Metaphorical Basis of Selfhood," in *Culture and Self: Asian and Western Perspectives*, ed. Anthony J. Marsella, George Devos, and Francis L. K. Hsu (New York: Tavistock Publications, 1985).

29. Carol Gilligan, *In a Different Voice: Psychological Theory and Women's Development* (Cambridge: Harvard University Press, 1982); Jean Baker Miller, *Towards a New Psychology of Women* (Boston: Beacon Press, 1977); Anne Wilson Schaef, *Women's Reality: An Emerging Female System in the White Male's Society* (Minneapolis: Winston Press, 1981); Ann Belford Ulanov, *Receiving Woman: Studies in the Psychology and Theology of the Feminine* (Philadelphia: Westminster Press, 1981).

30. Nancy Chodorow, *Reproduction of Mothering: Psychoanalysis and Sociology of Gender* (Berkeley: University of California Press, 1978), p. 44.

31. Gilligan, *In a Different Voice: Psychological Theory and Women's Development*, p. 433.

32. Chodorow, *Reproduction of Mothering*, p. 167.

33. Ibid.

34. Joan Scanlon, "Research Proposal for Life Themes in the Wives of Roman Catholic Deacons," Northwestern University, unpublished dissertation, 1985, p. 11.

35. Ibid.

36. See Emma Justes, "The Pastoral Care of Women," unpublished manuscript.

37. John S. Dunne, *The Way of All the Earth: Experiments in Truth and Religion* (New York: Macmillan Publishing Co., 1972); David W. Augsburger, *Pastoral Counseling across Cultures* (Philadelphia: Westminster Press, 1986); Clifford Geertz, *The Interpretation of Cultures* (New York: Basic Books, 1973); Laura Bohannon (pseudonym, Eleanor Bowen Smith), *Return to Laughter: An Anthropological Novel* (Garden City, N.Y.: Doubleday, 1954).

38. Augsburger, *Pastoral Counseling across Cultures*, p. 17.

39. Dunne, *The Way of All the Earth*, p. 53.

40. Eleanor Bowen Smith, *Return to Laughter*, p. 291.

41. Augsburger, *Pastoral Counseling across Cultures*, p. 13.

42. Urban T. Holmes, *The Priest in Community* (New York: Seabury Press, 1978); Wise, *Religion in Illness and Health*, chap. 3, p. 42.

43. Hinkle, "The Living Human Experience across Cultures," in *At the Point of Need: Living Human Experience*, p. 188.

44. Ibid., p. 188.

45. Augsburger, *Pastoral Counseling across Cultures*, p. 30.

46. James B. Ashbrook, *The Human Mind and the Mind of God: Theolog-

ical Promise in Brain Research (Lanham, Md.: University Press of America, 1984); Charles V. Gerkin, *The Living Human Document: Revisioning Pastoral Counseling in a Hermeneutical Mode* (Nashville: Abingdon Press, 1984); Don S. Browning, *The Moral Context of Pastoral Care* (Philadelphia: Westminster Press, 1976); Justes, "The Pastoral Care of Women"; Edward P. Wimberly, *Pastoral Counseling and Spiritual Values: A Black Point of View* (Nashville: Abingdon Press, 1982); Donald Capps, *Pastoral Care and Hermeneutics* (Philadelphia: Fortress Press, 1984).

47. Ashbrook, *The Human Mind and the Mind of God*, p. 332.

48. Charles V. Gerkin, *Widening the Horizons* (Philadelphia: Westminster Press, 1986); Capps, *Pastoral Care and Hermeneutics*.

49. Donald Capps, *Life Cycle Theory and Pastoral Care* (Philadelphia: Fortress Press, 1983).

50. Ibid., pp. 13, 33.

51. Ibid., p. 48.

52. Ibid., p. 120.

53. Paul Hessert, "Innocence and Experience: Towards a Theology of Pastoral Care," in *At the Point of Need: Living Human Experience*, p. 138.

54. Ibid., p. 140.

55. Ibid.

56. Ibid., pp. 140–141.

57. Dunne, *The Way of All the Earth: Experiments in Truth and Religion*, p. 53.

58. Ibid., p. 54.

59. Wise, *Religion in Illness and Health*, p. 142.

Index

acceptance, 86–87
adolescence, 107
Althaus, Paul, 13
altruism, 55
anal stage, 101
anger, 86
anxiety, 49, 54, 92
Ashbrook, James B., 161
Augsburger, David W., 158–161, 167
authority, 85
autonomy, 52, 55–58, 65, 66, 101–102, 152
awareness, 47–51, 152
Babel, 148
Baillie, D. M., 59
Bali, 152
Barbour, Ian, 153
Becker, Ernest, 155
behavioral sciences, 131–133
Berger, Peter, 154
Blake, William, 164
Bohannon, Laura, 158, 159
Bonhoeffer, Dietrich, 21
Bornkamm, Gunther, 13
boundaries, ego, 43–44
Bowers, Margaretta, 135
brain functioning, 161
Browning, Don S., 161, 162
Brunner, Emil, 86
Bultmann, Rudolf, 13
Cadbury, Henry J., 67
Calvin, John, 19, 69
Capps, Donald, 161–163, 166, 167
Chodorow, Nancy, 156, 157
church, 4, 25, 46, 51, 73
Clinebell, Howard J., 155
clinical pastoral training, 133, 134
Come, Arnold B., 28
communication, 9–26, 32, 43, 49, 56, 66, 69, 72, 81, 82
community, 44–46, 100, 112, 145

complex, 103
confession, 70, 74, 75
conflict, 54, 55
conformity, 57
confrontation, 30
conscience, 104
context, 141–142
conversation, 64–67, 148–151
counseling, 64, 70, 71, 74–75, 111
creation, 19, 20
crisis, 69, 71, 89, 96, 97
culture, 57, 58, 81, 111, 139, 141–170
defenses, 44, 55, 77, 93
dependence, 65
despair, 110, 120
determinism, 52, 84
dialogue, 66
didache, 12
Dillistone, F. W., 29
disgust, 110
distantiation, 109
doctrine, 17, 18, 41
doubt, 101–102, 116
drives, 90
Dunne, John S., 158, 159, 165, 166
education, 73
ego, 43, 53–56, 90, 92–96, 101, 110, 111
Electra, 103
elimination, 101
empathy, 14
encounter, 30
Erikson, Erik, 44, 91–116, 119, 120, 135, 158, 162
Eros, 90
evil, 119
"face," 151
family, 114
fantasy, 92
fellowship, 45
feminism, 156

Also from Meyer•Stone Books...

JESUS THE THERAPIST

Hanna Wolff

Hanna Wolff has spent nearly twenty years in psychotherapeutic practice, and in the course of treating her patients has looked for answers to their questions in the person and words of Jesus. Jesus, says Wolff, confronts human beings with the authentic humane person that *he himself was.* He thereby awakens people's own capacity for a humanness that is genuinely humane. Jesus makes a direct and immediate appeal to people to respond to their potential — to become what they can and ought to be. This spontaneous, direct grasp of people, this call to be *fully* human both startles and empowers us. And, says Wolff, it is in this calling forth of the authentic human that Jesus models for us the work of the therapist.

"Hanna Wolff sees deeply into the person and teaching of Jesus of Nazareth, in whom she sees a physician of the soul, and in whose teachings she sees spiritual and psychological counsel that is as alive today as it was some 2,000 years ago. . . . She has a remarkable capacity to move from the broadest and most searching spiritual principles to the most concrete and practical life-applications. She makes Jesus' teaching come alive through vignettes of her patient's lives. . . and nourishes not only the mind but also the soul."   *— John A. Sanford*

Hanna Wolff was born in Essen, Germany, in 1910. She studied theology in Tübingen and Jungian psychology in Zurich. Her first ministry was in the Pomeranian Confessing Church, and she spent many years working in India and Bolivia. She is the author of three other books and has been a practicing psychotherapist since 1969.

Theology/Psychology   192 pp.

Paperback: $12.95 (ISBN 0-940989-10-7)

SPEAK THAT WE MAY KNOW
A Spirituality for Uttering the Inner You

Justus George Lawler

"Simply to experience myself as *being* is to feel the being of all there is, the mystery that being is. And no one who has ever had this experience will ask what is the use of it. But how do we have this experience? That is what this book is about. The question is not 'How do I get it?' but rather 'How am I getting it, now, without realizing it?' Justus George Lawler has a fine knack for pointing up the looseners of our compact triviality, the primary one of which is language. And on the potential surprises and revelation in language, Lawler is second to no author I know."
— *Sebastian Moore*

"Justus George Lawler's book rings and sounds to the depths and across the breadth of the experience of speech. The acknowledgement of the depths of self-disclosure available in speech and the vulnerability that implies is not comfortable for us...but for any preacher who seeks to speak from heart to heart, deep calling to deep, this book provides an arena in which to take the risk."
— *Michael C. Williams, Director of Preaching Ministries, General Board of Discipleship, United Methodist Church*

Justus George Lawler is Professor of Humanities at St. Xavier College in Chicago. He is the author of many books, including *Celestial Pantomime*, and has published widely in journals such as *Worship*, *Psychiatry*, and *Thought*.

Spirituality   96 pp.

Paperback: $7.95 (ISBN 0-940989-41-7)

Order from your bookstore
or from
Meyer • Stone Books
2014 South Yost Avenue,
Bloomington, IN 47403
Tel.: 800-937-0313